MICHELLE TURNER

Gourmia Digital Air Fryer Cookbook 2023

1200-Day Quick & Easy Recipes For Beginners and Advanced Users | Air Fry, Bake, Dehydrate, and Rotisserie Mouthwatering Homemade Meals

First edition

This book was professionally typeset on Reedsy.
Find out more at reedsy.com

Contents

1

INTRODUCTION

Exactly How the Gourmia Air Fryer Works Deep frying adds a wonderful taste to food but also diminishes its nutritional content due to the high temperature at which it is cooked. When you fried something at high temperatures, the oil itself oxidizes, and then you add your food, which also absorbs the oil and loses all of its nutritional value. Damaged and oxidized oil plays a significant role in the development of cardiovascular disease. Air fryers, on the other hand, cook food uniformly by circulating hot air around the container, so ensuring that it cooks on all sides. Don't worry about uneven cooking; as long as your food doesn't become too packed in there, it'll cook properly on all sides. That's it, a tiny convection oven, right? There's something missing from that. Since the air in an air fryer circulates much more quickly than in an oven, and the appliance is sealed, cooking times and temperatures inside of it are altered. The Maillard effect, a surface-level reaction between amino acids and sugars that occurs between 280- and 330-degrees Fahrenheit, is responsible for the resulting crisp browning. Seared beef with a caramelized crust or a perfectly browned pie crust is a visual treat in addition to being delicious.

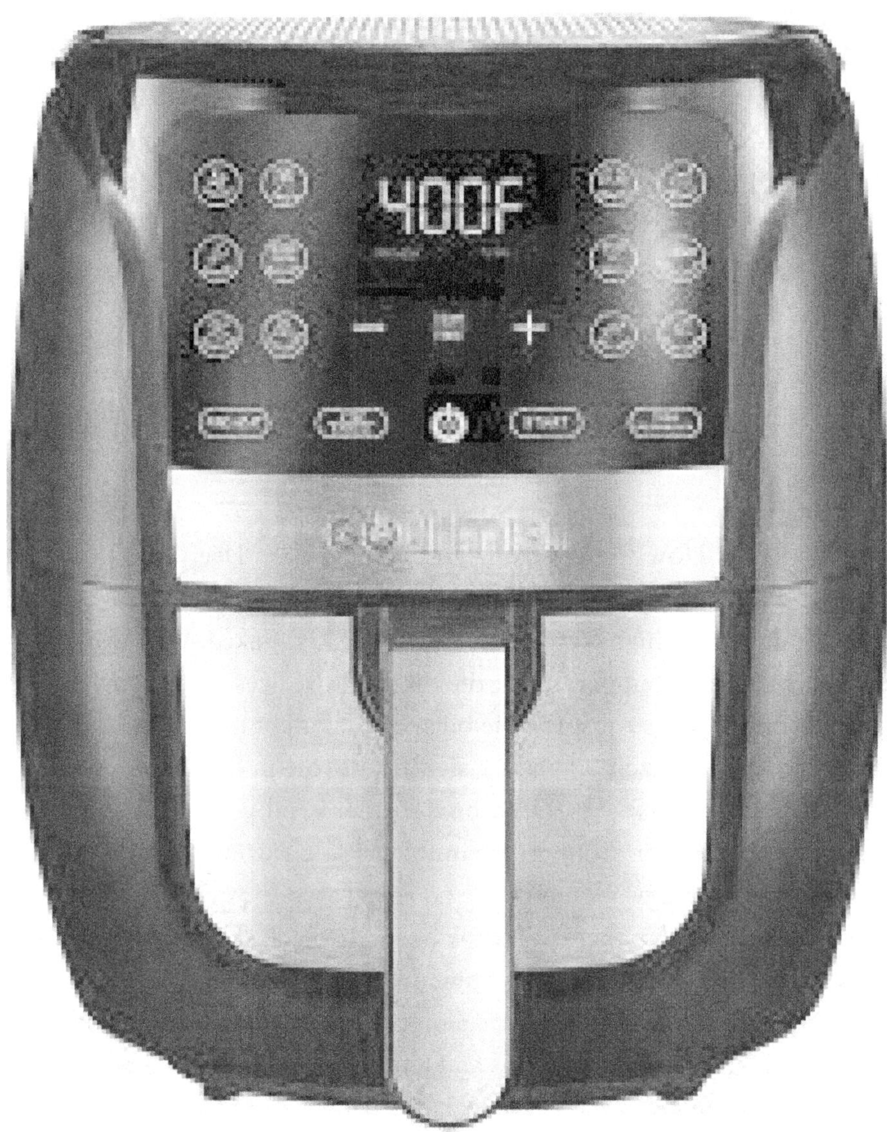

Whether by deep frying, grilling, or roasting, the Maillard reaction can occur in any food cooked at a temperature above the reaction's threshold. It's important to note that these methods aren't perfect. Heterocyclic amines (HCAs) and polycyclic aromatic hydrocarbons (PAHs) are formed when food is cooked at very high temperatures (PAH). By reading this, you'll get knowledge about those chemicals and the measures you can take to avoid contact with them in the future. Holding the surface temperature down to around 320 degrees Fahrenheit will prevent the formation of those hazardous chemicals. What's more, the health benefits of healthy fats are retained even when they're cooked at lower temperatures because these fats are resistant to oxidation.

Benefits of the Gourmia Air Fryer

Foods low in calories

Using a hot air fryer to cook your food will not add many more calories. While there may be times when taking extra calories is helpful, doing so is never recommended. If you use this appliance, your food will always be prepared in a healthy way and free of harmful fats. If you're overweight and have trouble maintaining a healthy weight, reducing the quantity of calories you consume daily may assist.

Little to no oil

While air frying, the food's inherent oils will be released, without the need for any additional oil. The hot air fryer works best with dry, grease-free food. Using a traditional deep fryer, where the food is bathed in oil throughout the cooking process, is a much less nutritious option. Burning oil creates byproducts that have been shown in studies to increase the risk of cancer and cardiovascular problems like heart failure. In addition, you'll save money on oil, and cutting costs anywhere you can is always a good idea.

Easy to use

Because of how easy it is to use, a hot air fryer allows anyone with little training or experience in the kitchen to make delicious meals. It's the biggest thing to happen to the food-preparation industry since microwave ovens, and that's saying a lot. Putting food inside and turning on the machine is all that's left to do. This appliance can help you save a lot of time in the kitchen because of how rapidly it prepares food. Use of a hot air fryer is not only practical, but also safe, thanks to a safety mechanism that immediately turns off the heating source in the event of a fire.

Easy to clean

There will be no slick to clean up if there is no oil to spill. Especially if you utilize your hot air fryer to make healthier options, such baked goods, or if you just want to eat less fatty foods, this will be the case. Also, even if things get dirty owing to the amount of food, they are easy to clean up. After a quick wipe off, it will look as good as new, saving you time and effort on the rest of the dishes.

Using the greatest hot air fryers, such as the HD9641, you can lock in the dish's wholesome flavor while keeping the oil temperature low enough to prevent the food from scorching. When food is torched and then cooked in oil, hazardous chemical compounds are produced. The nutrients are lost because they are either diluted in the oil or fragmented during the process. You may avoid this by using hot air frying, which will help keep your food from being overly greasy while keeping the flavor intact. The resulting cuisine is crisp and delicious.

Five Gourmia Air Fryer Tips for Beginners

To help you get started with your new air fryer, I have compiled a list of five tips and tricks that I think would be helpful.

Preheat Your Gourmia Air Fryer

It will only take you three minutes, but it will greatly enhance a wide variety of meals. This won't make much of a difference in certain recipes, but others, like oven-baked French toast, salmon, poultry, or veggies, will taste considerably better. Food's natural juices and moisture can be preserved by "searing" it on a heated surface. With other recipes, it is not as crucial because you can always add more time to the cooking process, but it is still a good idea to make it a habit to preheat the oven.

Avoid Cooking Sprays

Air fryer baskets include a non-stick coating on the inside, making cleanup a breeze. Avoid using cooking sprays on your stove top and other surfaces. Brush the surface of the basket with up to one teaspoon of oil to keep food from sticking, or toss the food in a tiny amount of high-heat oil (such as avocado oil, grapeseed oil, or sunflower oil). The usage of an oil mister bottle allows you to lightly coat your food with oil.

Don't Overcrowd The Air Fryer Basket

Refrain from the urge to overfill the basket in an effort to squeeze in a few more things. The result will be an unappetizing combination of raw and overcooked components in the cuisine. One of the most useful features of an air fryer is the ability to interrupt the frying process at any time. To ensure the food is being cooked uniformly, take out the basket, give it a gentle shake, and put it back in the oven.

Use Recipe Cooking Times As A Guide

I strongly advise getting a meat thermometer with a digital readout. Recipes should be used as a guide, but a thermometer is the only foolproof way to ensure that your food is cooked thoroughly. Due to the wide range of shapes and sizes available, the cooking time in an air fryer may be shorter or longer than what is called for in the recipe you're using.

Keep Your Gourmia Air Fryer Clean

Be sure to give the basket and the tray underneath a thorough cleaning after each usage. If you want to know if your air fryer can be washed in the dishwasher, look at the manual that came with it. You can't always throw your air fryer in the dishwasher to get it clean. In my experience, it's not hard to keep mine clean. When there's food stuck to the basket, I fill it halfway with hot water, add a few drops of dish soap, and let it soak for a few minutes before wiping it clean.

Cleaning the Interior of the Gourmia Air Fryer

It is crucial to wipe down the inside of the air fryer after each use in order to keep it sanitary. That way, you won't have to worry about making a huge mess. The majority of kitchen messes can be traced back to the grease that splatters everywhere while you prepare dinner. It's a popular myth that oven cleaner may be used in an air fryer, however if you do so, the scents from your air fryer will never go away, therefore DON'T DO IT!

Despite the claims of certain food writers, the use of soap inside the dishwasher will leave a distinct soapy flavor in your dishes for several washes.

There are two options for cleaning grease from the interior of my air fryer, and both work well.

In a shallow dish, combine one cup of water and two teaspoons of fresh lemon juice. Blend ingredients together by stirring. After that, put it in an air fryer and cook for three minutes at 300 degrees. As a result, the dirt will loosen off the walls, and cleaning the interior will be a breeze once everything has cooled down. The temperature needs to be checked to make sure everything is safe to handle.

Make a paste with the water and baking soda if the stains are particularly stubborn. The device's inner workings should then be cleansed with the solution.

2

POULTRY RECIPES

Turkey Bacon With Scrambled Eggs

Servings: 4

Cooking: 25 Minutes

Ingredients:

- 1 bell pepper, finely chopped
- 2 green onions, finely chopped
- 1/2 pound turkey bacon
- 4 eggs
- 1/3 cup milk
- 2 tablespoons yogurt
- 1/2 teaspoon sea salt
- 1/2 cup Colby cheese, shredded

Instructions

1. The turkey bacon should be placed in the cooking basket.
2. Cook at 360 degrees Fahrenheit for nine to eleven minutes. Work in groups. Hold the cooked bacon back.

3. In a mixing dish, whisk together the eggs, milk, and yogurt. Add salt, bell pepper, and green onions.
4. Coat the edges and bottom of the baking dish with the 1 teaspoon of bacon oil that was set aside.
5. The egg mixture is poured into the baking dish. 5 minutes at 3 degrees Fahrenheit. Add Colby cheese and simmer for an additional 5 to 6 minutes.
6. Enjoy the scrambled eggs with the bacon that was set aside.

Spicy Honey Orange Chicken

Servings: 4

Cooking: 20 Minutes

Ingredients:

- ½ cup orange marmalade
- 1 tbsp red pepper flakes
- ¼ cup honey
- 1 cup coconut, shredded
- ¾ cup breadcrumbs
- 2 whole eggs, beaten
- ½ cup flour
- ½ tsp pepper
- Salt to taste
- 3 tbsp dijon mustard

Instructions

1. Preheat air fryer to 400 degrees Fahrenheit. Combine coconut, flour, salt, and pepper in a mixing bowl. In another basin, whisk the eggs. Put breadcrumbs in a separate bowl. Coat chicken with an egg mixture, then flour, and then breadcrumbs. Place the chicken in the cooking basket of an air fryer and bake for minutes.

2. Mix honey, orange marmalade, mustard, and pepper flakes in a separate bowl. Cover chicken with the marmalade mixture and cook for an additional five minutes.

Juicy & Spicy Chicken Wings

Servings: 4

Cooking: 25 Minutes

Ingredients:

- 1 tsp Tabasco
- 2 lbs chicken wings
- 12 oz hot sauce
- 1 tsp Worcestershire sauce
- 6 tbsp butter, melted

Instructions

1. Spray the basket of an air fryer with cooking spray.
2. Cook chicken wings in the air fryer basket at 380 degrees Fahrenheit for many minutes. Shake basket after every 5 minutes.
3. Meanwhile, combine spicy sauce, Worcestershire sauce, and butter in a bowl. Set aside.
4. Add chicken wings to the sauce and combine thoroughly.
5. Serve with pleasure.

Almond Turkey And Shallots

Servings: 2

Cooking: 25 Minutes

Ingredients:

- 2 tablespoons olive oil

- 1 tablespoon sweet paprika
- 1 big turkey breast, skinless, boneless and halved
- 1/3 cup almonds, chopped
- Salt and black pepper to the taste
- 2 shallots, chopped

Instructions

1. In an air fryer-compatible pan, combine the turkey with the remaining ingredients, toss, and cook at 370 degrees Fahrenheit for 25 minutes. To serve, divide everything amongst plates.

Tasty Caribbean Chicken

Servings: 8
Cooking: 10 Minutes
Ingredients:

- 1 tbsp cayenne
- 1 tbsp cinnamon
- Pepper
- 3 lbs chicken thigh, skinless and boneless
- 1 tbsp coriander powder
- 3 tbsp coconut oil, melted
- ½ tsp ground nutmeg
- ½ tsp ground ginger
- Salt

Instructions

1. In a small bowl, combine all of the spices, then rub them all over the chicken.
2. Spray the basket of an air fryer with cooking spray.

3. Place chicken in the air fryer basket and cook for ten minutes at 0 degrees Fahrenheit.
4. Serve with pleasure.

Duck Legs And Scallions Mix

Servings: 2

Cooking: 16 Minutes

Ingredients:

- 1 teaspoon salt
- 2 duck legs
- 1 teaspoon olive oil
- ½ teaspoon ground cumin
- 1 tablespoon scallions, chopped

Instructions

1. In the small bowl, combine cumin powder and salt. Then, massage the spice mixture into the duck legs. Then, combine the scallions and olive oil. Sprinkle the scallion mixture over the duck legs. Preheat the air fryer to 385 degrees Fahrenheit. Place the duck legs in the air fryer for eight minutes. The duck legs are then flipped and cooked for an additional 8 minutes.

Thai Red Duck With Candy Onion

Servings: 4

Cooking: 25 Minutes

Ingredients:

- 1 tablespoon Thai red curry paste
- 1 cup candy onions, halved

- 1 ½ pounds duck breasts, skin removed
- 1 teaspoon kosher salt
- 1/2 teaspoon cayenne pepper
- 1/3 teaspoon black pepper
- 1/2 teaspoon smoked paprika
- 1/4 small pack coriander, chopped

Instructions

1. Place the duck breasts between two sheets of foil, and then use a rolling pin to pound them to a thickness of one inch.
2. Heat the Air Fryer to 395 degrees Fahrenheit.
3. Rub salt, cayenne pepper, black pepper, paprika, and red curry paste into the duck breasts. The duck breast should be placed in the cooking basket.
4. Cook between 11 and 12 minutes. Add candied onions and simmer for an additional 10 to 11 minutes.
5. Serve with coriander garnish and enjoy!

Leftovers 'n Enchilada Bake

Servings: 3
Cooking: 45 Minutes
Ingredients:

- 1-1/2 teaspoons vegetable oil
- 2 tablespoons cream cheese
- 2 tablespoons water
- 2-1/4 teaspoons chili powder
- 1 egg
- 1/2 (15 ounce) can black beans, drained
- 1/2 (15 ounce) can tomato sauce
- 1/2 (7.5 ounce) package corn bread mix

- 1/2 cup shredded Mexican-style cheese blend, or more to taste
- 1/2 envelope taco seasoning mix
- 1/2-pound chicken breast tenderloins
- 3 tablespoons milk

Instructions

1. Grease the air fryer's baking pan lightly with vegetable oil. Add chicken and fry at 360°F for 5 minutes per side.
2. Add chili powder, taco seasoning mix, water, and tomato sauce to the pan. Cook the chicken for 10 minutes, tossing and rotating it halfway through cooking.
3. Take the chicken out of the pan and shred it using two forks. Add cream cheese and black beans to the pan and stir. Blend well.
4. Mexican cheese should be used as a garnish
5. In a bowl, thoroughly whisk egg and milk. Mix in corn bread mix thoroughly. Pour over poultry.
6. Cover the dish with foil.
7. Continue cooking for 15 minutes. Remove the foil and bake for a further 10 minutes, or until the topping is lightly browned.
8. Let it rest for 5 minutes.
9. Serve with pleasure.

Bacon Wrapped Chicken Breasts

Servings: 4
Cooking: 23 Minutes
Ingredients:

- 1 tablespoon palm sugar
- Salt and ground black pepper, as required
- 6-7 Fresh basil leaves
- 2 tablespoons water

- 2 (8-ounces) chicken breasts, cut each breast in half horizontally
- 12 bacon strips
- 2 tablespoons fish sauce
- 1½ teaspoons honey

Instructions

1. Preheat the Air fryer to 365 degrees Fahrenheit and oil the basket.
2. In a small saucepan with a heavy bottom, caramelize the palm sugar over medium-low heat for approximately three minutes.
3. Stir in the basil, fish sauce, and water, then transfer the mixture to a bowl.
4. Salt and black pepper each chicken breast, then coat with the palm sugar mixture.
5. Refrigerate for approximately six hours, then wrap each piece of chicken with three bacon slices.
6. Dip in honey, then place in the Air Fryer basket.
7. Cook for approximately 20 minutes, turning once.
8. Serve the dish hot on a serving tray.
9. Refrigerate for approximately 4 to 6 hours to marinate.

Sweet Garlicky Chicken

Servings: 4
Cooking: 14 Minutes
Ingredients:

- ½ cup pineapple juice
- ½ cup soy sauce
- ¼ cup sesame oil
- 4 scallions, chopped
- 2 teaspoons sesame seeds, toasted
- 1 pound chicken tenders

- Wooden skewers, as required
- 1 tablespoon fresh ginger, grated finely
- 4 garlic cloves, minced
- Pinch of black pepper

Instructions

1. Prepare the Air fryer to 390 degrees Fahrenheit and grease the basket.
2. Except for the chicken, combine all the ingredients in a large baking dish.
3. Thread chicken onto skewers, then transfer them to a roasting tray.
4. Cover with marinade and refrigerate for approximately 3 hours.
5. Transfer half of the chicken skewers to the basket of the Air fryer and cook for approximately seven minutes.
6. Repeat with the remaining skewers and serve immediately while still warm.

Agave Mustard Glazed Chicken

Servings: 4
Cooking: 30 Minutes
Ingredients:

- 3 tablespoons agave syrup
- 1 tablespoon mustard
- 1 tablespoon avocado oil
- 2 pounds chicken breasts, boneless, skin-on
- 1 tablespoon Jamaican Jerk Rub
- 1/2 teaspoon salt
- 2 tablespoons scallions, chopped

Instructions

1. Begin by heating the Air Fryer to 370 degrees Fahrenheit.
2. Pour the avocado oil over the entire chicken breast. Then, apply the Jamaican Jerk rub to the chicken breast.
3. 15 minutes of cooking time in a hot Air Fryer. Cook them for a further 8 minutes after flipping.
4. In a pan over medium heat, combine the salt, agave syrup, and mustard while the chicken breasts are roasting. Allow the glaze to simmer until it thickens.
5. Then, brush the glaze over the entire chicken breast. Continue air-frying for six minutes, or until the surface is crisp. Serve with a garnish of fresh scallions. Bon appétit!

Hot Peppery Turkey Sandwiches

Servings: 4

Cooking: 25 Minutes

Ingredients:

- 3/4 teaspoon kosher salt
- 1/2 teaspoon ground black pepper
- 1 heaping tablespoon fresh cilantro, chopped
- A few dashes of Tabasco sauce
- 1 cup leftover turkey, cut into bite-sized chunks
- 2 bell peppers, deveined and chopped
- 1 Serrano pepper, deveined and chopped
- 1 leek, sliced
- 1/2 cup sour cream
- 1 teaspoon hot paprika
- 4 hamburger buns

Instructions

1. Except for the hamburger buns, put all items in an Air Fryer baking

tray until evenly coated.

2. Now, roast it at 385 degrees for minutes. Serve on hamburger buns; if preferred, add additional sour cream and Dijon mustard. Bon appétit!

Chicken Tenders With Parmesan And Lime

Servings: 6

Cooking: 20 Minutes

Ingredients:

- Sea salt and ground black pepper, to taste
- 1 teaspoon cayenne pepper
- 1/3 teaspoon ground cumin
- 1 teaspoon chili powder
- 1 lime
- 2 pounds chicken tenderloins, cut up
- 1/2 cup pork rinds, crushed
- 1/2 cup Parmesan cheese, grated
- 1 tablespoon olive oil
- 1 egg

Instructions

1. Apply lime juice to the entire bird.
2. Spray a nonstick cooking spray on the cooking basket.
3. Combine the pork rinds, Parmesan, olive oil, salt, black pepper, cayenne pepper, cumin, and chili powder in a mixing bowl.
4. In another small bowl, thoroughly whisk the egg. The chicken tenders are dipped in egg, then coated in pork rind mixture.
5. Transfer the breaded chicken to the cooking basket that has been prepared. Twelve minutes at 380 degrees Fahrenheit in a hot Air Fryer.
6. Flip them halfway through the cooking process. Work in groups. Serve without delay.

Turkey Rolls

Servings: 3

Cooking: 40 Minutes

Ingredients:

- Salt, to taste
- 2 tablespoons olive oil
- 3 tablespoons fresh parsley, finely chopped
- 1 pound turkey breast fillet
- 1 garlic clove, crushed
- 1½ teaspoons ground cumin
- 1 teaspoon ground cinnamon
- ½ teaspoon red chili powder
- 1 small red onion, finely chopped

Instructions

1. The turkey fillet is placed on a chopping board.
2. Cut horizontally along the length approximately one-third of the way from the top, stopping about one-fourth of an inch from the edge.
3. Open this section to obtain a lengthy fillet.
4. Combine the garlic, spices, and oil in a bowl.
5. Reserve roughly 1 tablespoon of the oil mixture in a small cup.
6. In the remaining oil mixture, thoroughly combine the parsley and onion.
7. Adjust the Air Fryer's temperature to 355 degrees Fahrenheit. Grease a basket for an Air Fryer.
8. Coat the fillet's exposed side with the onion mixture.
9. From the short side, tightly roll the fillet.
10. At 1-inch intervals, knot the roll with kitchen string.
11. Coat the exterior of the roll with the oil mixture that was prepared.
12. Arrange rolls in the Air Fryer's prepared basket.

13. Air-fry for roughly forty minutes.
14. Remove the turkey roll from the Air Fryer and leave it on a cutting board for 5 to 10 minutes before slicing.
15. Using a sharp knife, slice the turkey roll to the appropriate thickness and serve.

Eggs, Cauliflower ‘n Broccoli Brekky

Servings: 3

Cooking: 20 Minutes

Ingredients:

- ½ cup milk
- ½ cup shredded Cheddar cheese
- 1 cup broccoli, cut into little bits or riced
- 1 cup cauliflower, riced
- 1 teaspoons salt
- 1/2 teaspoon ground black pepper
- 1/2-pound hot pork sausage, diced
- 3 large eggs

Instructions

1. Spray the air fryer’s baking pan lightly with cooking spray. And cook pig sausage at 360 degrees for 5 minutes.
2. Remove basket and lightly toss the mixture. Add cauliflower and broccoli rice. Continue cooking for 5 minutes.
3. Whisk together eggs, salt, pepper, and milk. Stir in cheese.
4. Remove basket and pour in egg mixture.
5. Continue cooking for 10 minutes.
6. Serve with pleasure.

Bacon Chicken Mix

Servings: 2

Cooking: 25 Minutes

Ingredients:

- ½ teaspoon salt
- ½ teaspoon ground black pepper
- 2 chicken legs
- 4 oz bacon, sliced
- 1 teaspoon sesame oil

Instructions

1. Sprinkle chicken legs with salt and freshly ground black pepper, then wrap in bacon. Then, heat the air fryer to 385 degrees Fahrenheit. Sprinkle the chicken legs with sesame oil and place them in an air fryer. 25 minutes of cooking time should be allotted for the bacon-wrapped chicken legs.

Sweet Chili Chicken Wings

Servings: 4

Cooking: 20 Minutes

Ingredients:

- 1 tsp garlic powder
- 1 tbsp tamarind powder
- ¼ cup sweet chili sauce

Instructions

1. Preheat your Air Fryer to 390 degrees Fahrenheit. Spray the basket of

the air fryer with cooking spray.

2. Powder the chicken wings with tamarind and garlic. Coat the food with cooking spray and place in the cooking basket. Cook for 6 minutes, then cover with sweet chili sauce and cook for an additional 8 minutes. Serve chilled

Glazed Chicken Wings

Servings: 4

Cooking: 19 Minutes

Ingredients:

- 1 tablespoon soy sauce
- ½ teaspoon dried oregano, crushed
- 8 chicken wings
- 2 tablespoons all-purpose flour
- 1 teaspoon garlic, chopped finely
- 1 tablespoon fresh lemon juice
- Salt and freshly ground black pepper, to taste

Instructions

1. Prepare an Air fryer basket by greasing it and preheating the Air fryer to 355 degrees Fahrenheit.
2. Except for the wings, combine all ingredients in a large basin.
3. Coat the wings liberally with the marinade and refrigerate them for approximately two hours.
4. Remove the chicken wings from the marinade and evenly coat with flour.
5. Transfer the wings to the Air fryer tray and cook for approximately six minutes, turning once.
6. Serve the chicken wings piping hot on a plate.

Garlic Chicken Sausages

Servings: 4

Cooking: 10 Minutes

Ingredients:

- ½ teaspoon ground black pepper
- 4 sausage links
- 1 garlic clove, diced
- 1 spring onion, chopped
- 1 cup ground chicken
- ½ teaspoon salt
- 1 teaspoon olive oil

Instructions

1. Mix minced garlic, onion, ground chicken, salt, and ground black pepper in the mixing bowl. The sausage links are then stuffed with the ground chicken mixture. Cut each link of sausage in half and fasten the ends. Heat the air fryer to 365 degrees. Coat the sausages with olive oil, then place them in an air fryer. They should be cooked for a few minutes. Then flip the sausages and cook for a further 5 minutes. For quicker results, increase the cooking temperature to 390 degrees and cook for 8 minutes.

Chicken With Cashew Nuts

Servings: 4

Cooking: 30 Minutes

Ingredients:

- ⅓ cup cashew nuts, fried
- 1 capsicum, cut

- 2 tbsp garlic, crushed
- 2 tbsp soy sauce
- 1 tbsp cornflour
- 2 ½ cups onion cubes
- 1 carrot, chopped
- Salt and white pepper to taste

Instructions

1. Cubes of chicken should be marinated in a mixture of white pepper, salt, soy sauce, and cornstarch. Set aside for 25 minutes. Preheating the air fryer to 380 degrees Fahrenheit, place the marinated chicken inside. Add garlic, onion, bell pepper, and carrot, and cook for 5 to 6 minutes. Before serving, dredge it in cashew nuts.

Buttermilk Brined Turkey Breast

Servings: 8

Cooking: 20 Minutes

Ingredients:

- 1 fresh rosemary sprig
- ¾ cup brine from a can of olives
- 3½ pounds boneless, skinless turkey breast
- 2 fresh thyme sprigs
- ½ cup buttermilk

Instructions

1. Prepare an Air fryer basket by greasing it and preheating the Air fryer to 350 degrees Fahrenheit.
2. Olive brine and buttermilk should be thoroughly mixed in a bowl.
3. In a resealable plastic bag, combine the turkey breast, buttermilk

mixture, and herb sprigs.

4. Refrigerate the bag for approximately 12 hours.
5. Remove the turkey breast from the plastic bag and place it in the Air fryer basket.
6. Cook for approximately 20 minutes, turning once.
7. Dish the turkey breast onto a cutting board and slice to the desired thickness.

Crunchy Chicken Fingers

Servings: 2

Cooking: 8 Minutes

Ingredients:

- 2 tbsp plum sauce, optional
- ½ tbsp fresh thyme, chopped
- 3 tbsp Parmesan cheese
- ¼ tbsp fresh chives, chopped
- ⅓ cup breadcrumbs
- 1 egg white
- 1 tbsp water

Instructions

1. Preheat air fryer to 360 degrees Fahrenheit. Mix breadcrumbs, chives, Parmesan cheese, and thyme. In a separate bowl, whisk the egg white and water together. The chicken strips are dipped in the egg and breadcrumb mixtures. Place the strips in the basket of the air fryer and cook for several minutes. Prepare with a plum sauce.

Chicken And Scallion Kabobs

Servings: 4

Cooking: 24 Minutes

Ingredients:

- 1 tablespoon mirin
- 1 teaspoon garlic salt
- 4 (4-ounces) skinless, boneless chicken thighs, cubed into 1-inch size
- 2 bell peppers, cut into 1-inch pieces lengthwise
- Wooden skewers, presoaked
- ¼ cup light soy sauce
- 1 teaspoon sugar

Instructions

1. Prepare an Air fryer pan by greasing it and preheating the Air fryer to 355 degrees Fahrenheit.
2. In a large baking dish, combine the soy sauce, mirin, garlic salt, and sugar together.
3. Chicken and bell peppers are threaded onto wet wooden skewers.
4. Marinate the skewers in the refrigerator for approximately three hours.
5. Transfer the skewers in a single layer to the Air fryer pan and cook for approximately 12 minutes.
6. Warmly serve the dish on a plate.

Chicken Bbq With Sweet 'n Sour Sauce

Servings: 6

Cooking: 40 Minutes

Ingredients:

- ¼ cup minced garlic

- ¼ cup tomato paste
- ¾ cup minced onion
- ¾ cup sugar
- 1 cup soy sauce
- 1 cup water
- 1 cup white vinegar
- 6 chicken drumsticks
- Salt and pepper to taste

Instructions

1. Put all of the ingredients in a Ziploc bag.
2. Refrigerate the marinade for at least several hours.
3. Preheat the air fryer to 0 degrees Fahrenheit.
4. Insert the auxiliary grill pan into the air fryer.
5. The chicken is grilled for forty minutes.
6. Turn the chicken after 10 minutes to ensure consistent cooking.
7. Pour the marinade into a saucepan and cook it over medium heat until it thickens.
8. Before serving, apply the glaze on the chicken.

Cream Cheese Chicken Mix

Servings: 4

Cooking: 16 Minutes

Ingredients:

- ½ teaspoon smoked paprika
- ½ teaspoon ground nutmeg
- 1-pound chicken wings
- ¼ cup cream cheese
- 1 tablespoon apple cider vinegar
- 1 teaspoon Truvia

- 1 teaspoon avocado oil

Instructions

1. Cream cheese, Truvia, apple cider vinegar, smoked paprika, and ground nutmeg are combined in the mixing bowl. Then, add the chicken wings to the cream cheese mixture and coat them thoroughly. Allow the chicken to marinade in the cream cheese mixture for -15 minutes. Preheat the air fryer to 380 degrees Fahrenheit. Cook the chicken wings in an air fryer for eight minutes. Then, turn the wings over and coat them with cream cheese marinade. Cook the chicken wings for an additional 8 minutes.

Marjoram Chicken

Servings: 2

Cooking: 1 Hr.

Ingredients:

- ½ tsp. red pepper flakes, crushed
- 2 tsp. marjoram
- 2 skinless, boneless small chicken breasts
- 2 tbsp. butter
- 1 tsp. sea salt
- ¼ tsp. lemon pepper

Instructions

1. Coat the chicken breasts with the remaining ingredients in a bowl. Set aside to marinate for 30 - 60 minutes.
2. Preheat the Air Fryer to 390 degrees Fahrenheit.
3. Cook for 20 minutes, turning once halfway through.
4. Check for doneness with a thermometer with an instant-read display.

Serve over jasmine rice.

Fried Chicken Halves

Servings: 4
Cooking: 75 Minutes
Ingredients:

- 1 teaspoon salt
- 16 oz whole chicken
- 1 tablespoon dried thyme
- 1 teaspoon ground cumin
- 1 tablespoon avocado oil

Instructions

1. The chicken is cut in half and then seasoned with dried thyme, cumin, and salt. Apply avocado oil to the chicken halves. Preheat the air fryer to 365 degrees Fahrenheit. Cook the chicken breast halves in an air fryer for 60 minutes. The chicken halves are then flipped and cooked for an additional few minutes.

Thyme And Okra Chicken Thighs

Servings: 4
Cooking: 30 Minutes
Ingredients:

- Zest of 1 lemon, grated
- 4 garlic cloves, minced
- 1 tablespoon thyme, chopped
- 4 chicken thighs, bone-in and skinless
- A pinch of salt and black pepper

- 1 cup okra
- ½ cup butter, melted
- 1 tablespoon parsley, chopped

Instructions

1. In a pan that fits your air fryer, melt half the butter over medium heat and brown the chicken thighs for two to three minutes per side. Toss in the remaining butter, okra, and remaining ingredients, place the pan in the air fryer, and cook at 370 degrees Fahrenheit for 20 minutes. Divide amongst plates and serve.

Traditional Chicken Teriyaki

Servings: 4
Cooking: 50 Minutes
Ingredients:

- 1 teaspoon ginger, peeled and grated
- 2 garlic cloves, minced
- 1/2 teaspoon salt
- 1/2 teaspoon ground black pepper
- 1 ½ pounds chicken breast, halved
- 1 tablespoon lemon juice
- 2 tablespoons Mirin
- 1/4 cup milk
- 2 tablespoons soy sauce
- 1 tablespoon olive oil
- 1 teaspoon cornstarch

Instructions

1. Place the chicken, lemon juice, Mirin, milk, soy sauce, olive oil, ginger,

and garlic in a large ceramic dish. Allow it to marinade in your refrigerator for 30 minutes.

2. The sides and bottom of the cooking basket should be sprayed with a nonstick cooking spray. Cook the chicken in a cooking basket at 370 degrees Fahrenheit for 10 minutes.
3. Turn the chicken over, baste with the leftover marinade, and cook for an additional four minutes. Reserve after tasting for doneness and seasoning with salt and pepper.
4. Combine the cornstarch and 1 teaspoon of water. Add the marinade to the hot skillet and cook for three minutes over medium heat. Now, whisk in the cornstarch slurry and boil the sauce until it thickens.
5. Pour the sauce over the chicken that has been set aside, and serve immediately.

Crispy Chicken Tenders

Servings: 3

Cooking: 30 Minutes

Ingredients:

- ½ cup all-purpose flour
- 1½ cups panko breadcrumbs
- ¼ cup Parmesan cheese, finely grated
- 2 tablespoons butter, melted
- 2 (6-ounces) boneless, skinless chicken breasts, pounded into ½-inch thickness and cut into tenders
- ¾ cup buttermilk
- 1½ teaspoons Worcestershire sauce, divided
- ½ teaspoon smoked paprika, divided
- Salt and ground black pepper, as required
- 2 large eggs

Instructions

1. Combine buttermilk, 34 teaspoon of Worcestershire sauce, 14 teaspoon of paprika, salt, and black pepper in a large bowl.
2. Refrigerate the chicken tenders overnight in the refrigerator.
3. In a separate bowl, combine the remaining paprika, flour, salt, and black pepper.
4. In a third bowl, mix the remaining Worcestershire sauce and eggs until thoroughly incorporated.
5. In a fourth bowl, combine panko, Parmesan, and butter thoroughly.
6. Remove the tenders from the bowl and dispose of the buttermilk.
7. Coat the chicken tenders with the flour mixture, then the egg mixture, and then the panko mixture.
8. Adjust the air fryer's temperature to 400 degrees Fahrenheit. Grease a basket for an air fryer.
9. Place chicken tenders in the prepared air fryer basket in two separate, single-layer batches.
10. Air-fry for 13 to 15 minutes, flipping once during the cooking process.
11. Transfer the chicken tenders from the air fryer to a serving plate.
12. Serve warm.

3

BEEF, PORK & LAMB RECIPES

Roast Beef With Buttered Garlic-celery

Servings: 8
Cooking: 1 Hour
Ingredients:

- 2 sticks of celery, sliced
- 3 tablespoons olive oil
- A bunch of fresh herbs of your choice
- 1 bulb of garlic, peeled and crushed
- 1 tablespoon butter
- 2 medium onions, chopped
- 2 pounds topside of beef
- Salt and pepper to taste

Instructions

1. Warm the air fryer for five minutes.
2. In an air fryer-compatible baking dish, combine all the ingredients and give them a thorough toss.

3. Place the dish in the air fryer and bake for one hour at 0 degrees Fahrenheit.

Top Round Roast With Mustard-rosemary-thyme Blend

Servings: 10

Cooking: 1 Hour

Ingredients:

- 4 teaspoons dried oregano
- 4 teaspoons dried thyme
- 1 teaspoon dry mustard
- 2 teaspoons dried rosemary
- 3 tablespoons olive oil
- 4 pounds beef top round roast
- Salt and pepper to taste

Instructions

1. Warm the air fryer for five minutes.
2. Place all ingredients in an air fryer-compatible baking dish.
3. Cook the food in an air fryer for one hour at 50 degrees Fahrenheit.Warm the air fryer for five minutes.
4. Place all ingredients in an air fryer-compatible baking dish.
5. Cook the food in an air fryer for one hour at 50 degrees Fahrenheit.

Smoked Pork

Servings: 5

Cooking: 20 Minutes

Ingredients:

- 1 tablespoon olive oil

- 1-pound pork shoulder
- 1 tablespoon liquid smoke
- 1 teaspoon salt

Instructions

1. In the shallow bowl, combine liquid smoke, salt and olive oil. Then, carefully brush each side of the pork shoulder with the liquid smoke mixture. Cut the meat into little pieces. Preheat the air fryer to 390 degrees Fahrenheit. Place the pork shoulder in the basket of the air fryer and cook the meat for several minutes. After this, turn the meat and cook for an additional 10 minutes. Rest the pork shoulder for 10 to 15 minutes after cooking. Utilize 2 forks to shred the item.

Beef, Lettuce And Cabbage Salad

Servings: 4

Cooking: 25 Minutes

Ingredients:

- ½ green cabbage head, shredded
- 2 tablespoons almonds, sliced
- 1 tablespoon sesame seeds
- ½ tablespoon white vinegar
- 1 pound beef, cubed
- ¼ cup coconut aminos
- 1 tablespoon coconut oil, melted
- 6 ounces iceberg lettuce, shredded
- 2 tablespoons cilantro, chopped
- 2 tablespoons chives, chopped
- 1 zucchini, shredded
- A pinch of salt and black pepper

Instructions

1. In a pan that fits an air fryer, heat the oil over medium heat and brown the meat for 5 minutes. Add the aminos, zucchini, cabbage, salt, and pepper, stir, and fry at 370 degrees Fahrenheit for twenty minutes. Transfer the mixture to a salad bowl, add the remaining ingredients, stir, and serve.

Caraway, Sichuan 'n Cumin Lamb Kebabs

Servings: 3
Cooking: 1 Hour
Ingredients:

- 2 teaspoons caraway seeds, toasted
- 2 teaspoons crushed red pepper flakes
- 1 ½ pounds lamb shoulder, bones removed and cut into pieces
- 1 tablespoon Sichuan peppercorns
- 1 teaspoon sugar
- 2 tablespoons cumin seeds, toasted
- Salt and pepper to taste

Instructions

1. Place all ingredients in a bowl and marinate the meat in the refrigerator for at least two hours.
2. Preheat the air fryer to 3900 degrees Fahrenheit.
3. Insert the auxiliary grill pan into the air fryer.
4. Per batch, grill the meat for 15 minutes.
5. Turn the meat every 8 minutes to ensure equal cooking.

Beef Schnitzel

Servings: 1

Cooking: 30 Minutes

Ingredients:

- 2 tbsp. olive oil
- 1 parsley, roughly chopped
- 1 egg
- 1 thin beef schnitzel
- 3 tbsp. friendly bread crumbs
- ½ lemon, cut in wedges

Instructions

1. Preheat your Air Fryer to 360°F in advance.
2. Mix the bread crumbs and olive oil in a bowl to produce a loose, crumbly mixture.
3. Whisk the egg using a whisk.
4. Coat the schnitzel first in the egg, then in the bread crumbs, making sure to completely cover it.
5. In the Air Fryer, fry the schnitzel for 12 to 14 minutes. Before serving, garnish the schnitzel with the lemon wedges and parsley.

Pork Chops And Sage Sauce Recipe

Servings: 2

Cooking: 25 Minutes

Ingredients:

- 2 tbsp. butter
- 2 pork chops
- 1 shallot; sliced

- 1 handful sage; chopped
- Salt and black pepper to the taste
- 1 tbsp. olive oil
- 1 tsp. lemon juice

Instructions

1. Season pork chops with salt and pepper, rub with oil, place in an air fryer, and cook at 370 degrees Fahrenheit for minutes, turning them halfway through cooking.
2. In the meantime, melt the butter in a pan over medium heat, add the shallot, and cook while stirring for a few minutes.
3. Add sage and lemon juice; stir well, cook a few minutes longer, then remove from heat.
4. Serve pork chops drizzled with sage sauce on individual plates.

Sausage Meatballs

Servings: 4

Cooking: 15 Minutes

Ingredients:

- 3 tablespoons Italian breadcrumbs
- ½ teaspoon garlic, minced
- 3½-ounce sausage, casing removed
- ½ medium onion, minced finely
- 1 teaspoon fresh sage, chopped finely
- Salt and black pepper, to taste

Instructions

1. Prepare an Air fryer basket by greasing it and preheating the Air fryer to 355 degrees Fahrenheit.

2. All the ingredients should be thoroughly mixed in a bowl.
3. Form the mixture into balls of equal size and place them in the Air fryer basket.
4. Cook for approximately 15 minutes and serve warm.

Cumin-paprika Rubbed Beef Brisket

Servings: 12

Cooking: 2 Hours

Ingredients:

- 2 teaspoons dry mustard
- 2 teaspoons ground black pepper
- 2 teaspoons salt
- 5 pounds brisket roast
- ¼ teaspoon cayenne pepper
- 1 ½ tablespoons paprika
- 1 teaspoon garlic powder
- 1 teaspoon ground cumin
- 1 teaspoon onion powder
- 5 tablespoons olive oil

Instructions

1. Place all ingredients in a Ziploc bag and marinate for at least two hours in the refrigerator.
2. Warm the air fryer for five minutes.
3. Place the meat in an air fryer-compatible baking dish.
4. Place in an air fryer and cook at 3500F for 2 hours.

Stuffed Bell Pepper

Servings: 4

Cooking: 25 Minutes

Ingredients:

- 1 tsp. garlic salt
- 2 tsp. Worcestershire sauce
- 8 oz. tomato sauce
- 2 garlic cloves, minced
- 4 bell peppers, cut top of bell pepper
- 16 oz. ground beef
- 2/3 cup cheese, shredded
- ½ cup rice, cooked
- 1 tsp. basil, dried
- ½ tsp. chili powder
- 1 tsp. black pepper
- 1 small onion, chopped

Instructions

1. In a skillet coated with cooking spray, sauté the onion and garlic over medium heat.
2. Mix together the beef, basil, chili powder, black pepper, and garlic salt thoroughly. Before removing the skillet from the heat, let the beef cook until it is beautifully browned.
3. Stir together half of the cheese, the rice, Worcestershire sauce, and tomato sauce.
4. Spoon equal portions of the meat mixture into each of the four bell pepper halves.
5. Pre-heat the Air Fryer to 400 degrees Fahrenheit.
6. Spray the basket of the Air Fryer with cooking spray.
7. Place the peppers in the basket and allow them to cook for 11 minutes.

8. Add the remaining cheese on top of each bell pepper and cook for an additional two minutes. As soon as the cheese has melted and the peppers are sizzling, serve immediately.

Monterey Jack'n Sausage Brekky Casserole

Servings: 2

Cooking: 20 Minutes

Ingredients:

- 1/4-lb breakfast sausage
- 2 tbsp red bell pepper, diced
- ½ cup shredded Cheddar-Monterey Jack cheese blend
- 1 green onion, chopped
- 1 pinch cayenne pepper
- 4 eggs

Instructions

1. Spray the air fryer's baking pan lightly with cooking spray.
2. Add sausage and cook at 390°F for 8 minutes. At the halfway point, shred sausage and mix thoroughly.
3. In the meantime, whisk eggs in a bowl and combine them with bell pepper, green onion, and cayenne.
4. Remove basket and lightly toss the mixture. On top of the cheese, pour eggs evenly.
5. Cook eggs for a further 12 minutes at 330 degrees Fahrenheit, or until desired doneness.
6. Serve with pleasure.

Grilled Prosciutto Wrapped Fig

Servings: 2
Cooking: 8 Minutes
Ingredients:

- 2 whole figs, sliced in quarters
- 8 prosciutto slices
- Pepper and salt to taste

Instructions

1. Wrap a slice of prosciutto around a slice of fid, then thread onto a skewer. Repeat the procedure with the remaining Ingredients. Place on the air fryer's skewer rack.
2. Cook for 8 minutes at 390°F. Halfway through the cooking process, rotate the skewers.
3. Serve with pleasure.

Coconut Pork And Green Beans

Servings: 4
Cooking: 25 Minutes
Ingredients:

- A pinch of salt and black pepper
- ½ pound green beans, trimmed and halved
- 4 pork chops
- 2 tablespoons coconut oil, melted
- 2 garlic cloves, minced
- 2 tablespoons keto tomato sauce

Instructions

1. In a pan that fits an air fryer, heat the oil over medium heat and brown the pork chops for five minutes. Add the other ingredients, place the pan in the oven, and cook at 390 degrees Fahrenheit for twenty minutes. Serve everything on separate plates.

Peppery Roasted Potatoes With Smoked Bacon

Servings: 2

Cooking: 15 Minutes

Ingredients:

- 1/3 teaspoon ground black pepper
- 1 bell pepper, seeded and sliced
- 1 teaspoon mustard
- 5 small rashers smoked bacon
- 1/3 teaspoon garlic powder
- 1 teaspoon sea salt
- 2 teaspoons paprika
- 2 habanero peppers, halved

Instructions

1. Simply combine all the ingredients in a mixing bowl, and then transfer them to the basket of your air fryer.
2. Air-fry for 10 minutes at 375 degrees Fahrenheit. Serve hot.

Steak With Cascabel-garlic Sauce

Servings: 4

Cooking: 20 Minutes

Ingredients:

- 2 teaspoons cumin seeds

- 3 cloves garlic, pressed
- Pink peppercorns to taste, freshly cracked
- 1 teaspoon fine table salt
- 2 teaspoons brown mustard
- 2 tablespoons mayonnaise
- 1 ½ pounds beef flank steak, trimmed and cubed
- 2 teaspoons minced cascabel
- ½ cup scallions, finely chopped
- 1/3 cup Crème fraîche
- 1/3 teaspoon black pepper, preferably freshly ground

Instructions

1. Fry the cumin seeds for a minute or until they begin to burst.
2. After seasoning the flank steak with fine table salt, black pepper, and fried cumin seeds, place the beef cubes on the bottom of an air fryer-compatible baking dish.
3. Add the minced cascabel, garlic, and scallions; air-fry at 0 degrees Fahrenheit for approximately 8 minutes.
4. Once the beef begins to get soft, add your preferred mayonnaise, crème fraîche, freshly cracked pink peppercorns, and mustard; air-fry for an additional seven minutes. Serve atop warm wild rice. Bon appétit!

Simple Garlic 'n Herb Meatballs

Servings: 4

Cooking: 20 Minutes

Ingredients:

- 1 teaspoon dried mixed herbs
- 1 clove of garlic, minced
- 1 egg, beaten
- 1 tablespoon breadcrumbs or flour

- 1-pound lean ground beef

Instructions

1. Put all the ingredients in a bowl and mix them with your hands.
2. Form little balls with your hands, then place them in the refrigerator to set.
3. Preheat the air fryer to 0 degrees Fahrenheit.
4. Cook the meatballs for 20 minutes in the air fryer basket.
5. Shake the meatballs halfway during the cooking time to ensure that they cook evenly.

Moroccan Beef Kebab

Servings: 4
Cooking: 30 Minutes
Ingredients:

- 3 saffron threads
- 2 tablespoons loosely packed fresh continental parsley leaves
- 4 tablespoons tahini sauce
- 4 ounces baby arugula
- 1/2 cup leeks, chopped
- 2 garlic cloves, smashed
- 2 pounds ground chuck
- Salt, to taste
- 1/4 teaspoon ground black pepper, or more to taste
- 1 teaspoon cayenne pepper
- 1/2 teaspoon ground sumac
- 1 tomato, cut into slices

Instructions

1. In a bowl, combine the chopped leeks, minced garlic, ground beef, and spices; knead until thoroughly combined.
2. Now, wrap the beef mixture around a wooden stick to form a sausage with a pointed end.
3. 25 minutes at 0 degrees Fahrenheit in the preheated Air Fryer.
4. Serve your kebab with arugula, tomato, and tahini sauce. Enjoy!

Pork With Balsamic-raspberry Jam

Servings: 4

Cooking: 30 Minutes

Ingredients:

- 2 tablespoons sugar
- 2/3 cup balsamic vinegar
- 4 smoked pork chops
- ¼ cup all-purpose flour
- ¼ cup milk
- 1 cup chopped pecans
- 1 cup panko breadcrumbs
- 2 large eggs, beaten
- 2 tablespoons raspberry jam
- Salt and pepper to taste

Instructions

1. Preheat the air fryer to 3300 degrees Fahrenheit.
2. Season pork chops to taste with salt and pepper.
3. Eggs and milk are whisked together in a small bowl. Set aside.
4. Coat the pork chops in flour, then the egg mixture, before dredging them in panko and pecans.
5. Prepare in an air fryer for thirty minutes.
6. Meanwhile, prepare the sauce by placing the remaining ingredients in

a saucepan. Salt and pepper are used as seasonings.

7. After cooking the pork chops, drizzle them with the sauce.

Herb-crusted Filet Mignon

Servings: 4

Cooking: 20 Minutes

Ingredients:

- 1 teaspoon dried thyme
- 1 tablespoon sesame oil
- 1 small-sized egg, well-whisked
- 1 pound filet mignon
- Sea salt and ground black pepper, to your liking
- 1/2 teaspoon cayenne pepper
- 1 teaspoon dried basil
- 1 teaspoon dried rosemary
- 1/2 cup parmesan cheese, grated

Instructions

1. Add salt, black pepper, cayenne pepper, basil, rosemary, and thyme to the filet mignon. Coat in sesame oil.
2. Place the egg on a shallow dish. Put the parmesan cheese on a separate plate.
3. Coat the filet mignon with egg, and then place it in the parmesan cheese. Set your Air Fryer to 0 degrees Fahrenheit.
4. 10 to 13 minutes, or until golden brown. Serve with a mixed salad and relish!

Scrumptious Lamb Chops

Servings: 4

Cooking: 8 Minutes

Ingredients:

- 1 garlic clove, minced
- 2 tablespoons dried rosemary
- 3 tablespoons olive oil
- 2 tablespoons fresh mint leaves, minced
- 4 (6-ounce) lamb chops
- 2 carrots, peeled and cubed
- 1 parsnip, peeled and cubed
- 1 fennel bulb, cubed
- Salt and black pepper, to taste

Instructions

1. Prepare the Air fryer to 390 degrees Fahrenheit and grease the basket.
2. In a large dish, combine the herbs, garlic, and oil, then liberally coat the pork chops with this mixture.
3. Marinate for hours in the refrigerator.
4. Soak the vegetables for approximately 15 minutes in a big pot of water.
5. Cook the chops in the Air fryer basket for approximately two minutes.
6. Remove the chops from the Air fryer basket and replace it with the vegetables.
7. Cook the chops for approximately 6 minutes.
8. Dispense and serve hot.

4

FISH & SEAFOOD RECIPES

Cheesy Shrimps

Servings: 4
Cooking: 5 Minutes
Ingredients:

- 4 oz Monterey jack cheese, shredded
- 14 oz shrimps, peeled
- 2 eggs, beaten
- ¼ cup heavy cream
- 1 teaspoon salt
- 1 teaspoon ground black pepper
- 5 tablespoons coconut flour
- 1 tablespoon lemon juice, for garnish

Instructions

1. Combine heavy cream, salt, and ground black pepper in the mixing bowl. Add eggs and whisk until the mixture is uniform. Then, combine coconut flour and Monterey jack cheese. Coat the shrimp with the

coconut flour mixture after dipping them in the heavy cream sauce. The shrimp are then dipped again in the egg mixture and coated with coconut flour. Preheat the air fryer to 400 degrees Fahrenheit. Cook the shrimp for five minutes in a single layer in an air fryer. Repeat this procedure with the remaining shrimp. The bang-bang shrimp should be seasoned with lemon juice.

Classic Parmesan Fish Fillets

Servings: 4
Cooking: 15 Minutes
Ingredients:

- Salt and ground black pepper, to taste
- 1 cup parmesan, grated
- 1 teaspoon garlic powder
- 1/2 teaspoon shallot powder
- 1 egg, well whisked
- 4 white fish fillets
- Fresh Italian parsley, to serve

Instructions

1. The parmesan should be placed in a small bowl.
2. Combine the garlic powder, shallot powder, and beaten egg in a separate bowl.
3. Season the fish fillets liberally with salt and pepper. Each fillet is dipped in the beaten egg.
4. The fillets are then rolled in the parmesan mixture. Set your Air Fryer to 370 degrees Fahrenheit. Air-fry for ten to twelve minutes.
5. Enjoy while garnished with fresh parsley!

Glazed Halibut

Servings: 3

Cooking: 15 Minutes

Ingredients:

- ¼ cup sugar
- ¼ teaspoon red pepper flakes, crushed
- 1 garlic clove, minced
- ¼ teaspoon fresh ginger, finely grated
- ½ cup cooking wine
- ½ cup low-sodium soy sauce
- ¼ cup fresh orange juice
- 2 tablespoons lime juice
- 1 pound halibut steak

Instructions

1. Bring the garlic, ginger, wine, soy sauce, juices, sugar, and red pepper flakes to a boil in a medium saucepan.
2. Cook for approximately 3 to 4 minutes, stirring constantly.
3. Remove the marinade from the heat and let it to cool.
4. Reserve half of the marinade in a small bowl in the refrigerator.
5. Place the leftover marinade and halibut steak in a resealable bag.
6. Close the bag and shake it vigorously to evenly distribute the coating.
7. Refrigerate for roughly thirty minutes.
8. Adjust the air fryer's temperature to 390 degrees Fahrenheit. Grease a basket for an air fryer.
9. Place halibut steak in the air fryer's prepared basket.
10. Air-fry for roughly 9 to 11 minutes.
11. Remove the halibut steak from the air fryer and lay it on a dish.
12. Cut the steak into three pieces of similar size and brush with the remaining glaze.

13. Serve without delay.

Summer Fish Packets

Servings: 2

Cooking: 20 Minutes

Ingredients:

- 1/4 teaspoon freshly ground black pepper
- 1/2 teaspoon paprika
- Sea salt, to taste
- 2 snapper fillets
- 1 shallot, peeled and sliced
- 2 garlic cloves, halved
- 1 bell pepper, sliced
- 1 small-sized serrano pepper, sliced
- 1 tomato, sliced
- 1 tablespoon olive oil
- 2 bay leaves

Instructions

1. Place two sheets of parchment on a work surface. Position the fish in the middle of one side of parchment paper.
2. Add the shallot, garlic, peppers, and tomato to the pizza. Olive oil should be drizzled over the fish and vegetables. Season with salt, black pepper, and paprika. Include bay leaves.
3. Fold the opposite half of the parchment over. Now, wrap the paper tightly around the edges to form a half moon and seal the fish within.
4. 15 minutes at 390 degrees Fahrenheit in the preheated Air Fryer. Serve hot.

Mustard Cod

Servings: 4
Cooking: 14 Minutes
Ingredients:

- 1 cup parmesan, grated
- 4 cod fillets, boneless
- Salt and black pepper to the taste
- 1 tablespoon mustard

Instructions

1. Stir together the parmesan, salt, pepper, and mustard in a bowl. Spread this over the cod, place the fish in the basket of the air fryer, and cook at 370 degrees Fahrenheit for seven minutes per side. Divide among plates and serve with a salad on the side.

Rosemary Garlic Prawns

Servings: 2
Cooking: 15 Minutes
Ingredients:

- 3 garlic cloves, minced
- 1 rosemary sprig, chopped
- ½ tbsp melted butter
- Salt and pepper, to taste

Instructions

1. In a bowl, combine garlic, butter, rosemary, salt, and pepper. Add the shrimp to the bowl and thoroughly coat them. Cover and chill the bowl

for one hour. Preheat the air fryer to 350 degrees Fahrenheit and cook for six minutes. Boost the temperature to 390 degrees and cook for an additional minute.

Honey Sea Bass Recipe

Servings: 2

Cooking: 20 Minutes

Ingredients:

- 2 oz. watercress
- A small bunch of parsley; chopped
- 2 sea bass fillets
- Zest from 1/2 orange; grated
- Juice from 1/2 orange
- 2 tbsp. mustard
- 2 tsp. honey
- 2 tbsp. olive oil
- 1/2 lb. canned lentils; drained
- A small bunch of dill; chopped
- A pinch of salt and black pepper

Instructions

1. Season fish fillets with salt and pepper, add orange zest and juice, rub with 1 tablespoon of oil, honey, and mustard, transfer to an air fryer, and cook at 350 degrees Fahrenheit for 10 minutes, turning halfway through.
2. In the meantime, place lentils in a small saucepan and warm them over medium heat. Add the remaining oil, watercress, dill, and parsley, and stir well. Add the fish fillets and serve immediately.

Gingery Cod Filet Recipe From Hong Kong

Servings: 2

Cooking: 15 Minutes

Ingredients:

- 5 slices of ginger
- A dash of sesame oil
- 2 cod fish fillets
- 250 mL water
- 3 tablespoons coconut aminos
- 3 tablespoons coconut oil
- Green onions for garnish

Instructions

1. Warm up the air fryer for five minutes.
2. In a baking dish, combine all ingredients except for the green onions.
3. Place in an air fryer and cook at 4000F for 15 minutes.
4. The dish is garnished with green onions.

Catfish Bites

Servings: 4

Cooking: 10 Minutes

Ingredients:

- 10 oz catfish fillet
- ¼ cup coconut flakes
- 3 tablespoons coconut flour
- 1 teaspoon salt
- 3 eggs, beaten
- Cooking spray

Instructions

1. Cut the fillet of catfish into small pieces (nuggets) and season with salt. Then, dunk the catfish pieces in egg and coat them with coconut flour. The fish pieces are then dipped in egg again and coated with coconut flakes. Preheat the air fryer to 385 degrees Fahrenheit. Place the catfish nuggets in the basket of the air fryer and cook for six minutes. Then, rotate the nuggets and cook for an additional four minutes.

Cajun Lemon Salmon

Servings: 1

Cooking: 15 Minutes

Ingredients:

- ¼ tsp. sugar
- 1 salmon fillet
- 1 tsp. Cajun seasoning
- ½ lemon, juiced
- 2 lemon wedges, for serving

Instructions

1. Pre-heat the Air Fryer to 350 degrees Fahrenheit.
2. Mix the lemon juice and sugar together.
3. The fish is coated with the sugar mixture.
4. Sprinkle the fish with Cajun spice.
5. Line the bottom of your deep fryer with parchment paper.
6. Allow the salmon to cook in the fryer for seven minutes.

Fish Fillets

Servings: 4

Cooking: 25 Minutes

Ingredients:

- 4 tbsp. olive oil
- 4 fish fillets
- 1 egg, beaten
- 1 cup bread crumbs
- Pepper and salt to taste

Instructions

1. Pre-heat the Air Fryer to 350 degrees Fahrenheit.
2. Combine the bread crumbs, oil, pepper, and salt in a shallow plate.
3. The beaten egg is poured into a second dish.
4. Before coating each fish fillet in bread crumbs, dredge it in the egg. Place in the basket of an Air Fryer.
5. Allow the Air Fryer to cook for 12 minutes.

Tuna Au Gratin With Herbs

Servings: 4

Cooking: 20 Minutes

Ingredients:

- 1/2 teaspoon dried rosemary
- 1/2 teaspoon dried basil
- 1/2 teaspoon dried thyme
- 2 small ripe tomatoes, pureed
- 1 tablespoon butter, melted
- 1 medium-sized leek, thinly sliced

- 1 tablespoon chicken stock
- 1 tablespoon dry white wine
- 1 pound tuna
- 1/2 teaspoon red pepper flakes, crushed
- Sea salt and ground black pepper, to taste
- 1 cup Parmesan cheese, grated

Instructions

1. In a sauté pan, melt 2 tablespoons of butter over medium heat. Now, sauté the leeks and garlic until they are soft and fragrant. Add the stock and wine to the pan to deglaze it.
2. Heat the Air Fryer to 370 degrees Fahrenheit.
3. The remaining 1/2 tablespoon of melted butter should be used to grease a casserole dish. Fish should be placed in the casserole dish. Add the condiments. Add the sautéed leek mixture on top.
4. Incorporate tomato puree. Air fry for ten minutes in a hot Air Fryer. Add Parmesan cheese gratings and bake for an additional 7 minutes, or until the crumbs are golden brown. Bon appétit!

Herbed Calamari Rings

Servings: 4

Cooking: 4 Minutes

Ingredients:

- 1 teaspoon butter, melted
- ¼ teaspoon ground coriander
- 1 chili pepper, chopped
- ¼ teaspoon salt
- 10 oz calamari
- ½ teaspoon dried cilantro
- ½ teaspoon dried parsley

- 1 teaspoon apple cider vinegar
- 1 teaspoon sesame oil

Instructions

1. Clean and trim the calamari. The onion is then sliced into rings and seasoned with salt, dried cilantro, coriander, and apple cider vinegar. Add sesame oil to the calamari rings and stir. Preheat the air fryer to 400 degrees Fahrenheit. Cook the calamari rings for two minutes in the air fryer basket. When the time is up, give them a good shake and cook for an additional two minutes. Place the calamari rings in a large bowl and dot with butter.

Fried Branzino

Servings: 4
Cooking: 20 Minutes
Ingredients:

- Juice from 1/2 lemon
- Juice from 1/2 orange
- 4 medium branzino fillets; boneless
- 1/2 cup parsley; chopped
- 2 tbsp. olive oil
- A pinch of red pepper flakes; crushed
- Zest from 1 lemon; grated
- Zest from 1 orange; grated
- Salt and black pepper to the taste

Instructions

1. In a large bowl, combine fish fillets with lemon zest, orange zest, lemon juice, orange juice, salt, pepper, oil, and pepper flakes; toss very well,

then transfer fillets to an air fryer prepared to 350 degrees Fahrenheit and bake for minutes, turning once. Plate the fish, sprinkle with parsley, and serve immediately.

Spicy Shrimp

Servings: 2
Cooking: 6 Minutes
Ingredients:

- 1/4 tsp paprika
- 1/2 lb shrimp, peeled and deveined
- 1/2 tsp old bay seasoning
- 1 tsp cayenne pepper
- 1 tbsp olive oil
- 1/8 tsp salt

Instructions

1. Preheat the air fryer to 390 degrees Fahrenheit.
2. Add all items to the bowl and combine them thoroughly.
3. Transfer shrimp to the basket of an air fryer and cook for six minutes.
4. Serve with pleasure.

Delicious Crab Cakes

Servings: 4
Cooking: 10 Minutes
Ingredients:

- 2 tbsp parsley, chopped
- 1/4 cup almond flour
- 1/4 tsp pepper

- 8 oz crab meat
- 2 tbsp butter, melted
- 2 tsp Dijon mustard
- 1 tbsp mayonnaise
- 1 egg, lightly beaten
- 1/2 tsp old bay seasoning
- 1 green onion, sliced
- 1/2 tsp salt

Instructions

1. In a mixing bowl, combine all ingredients except butter until well blended.
2. Make four patties from the mixture and set them on a platter lined with parchment paper.
3. Refrigerate the plate for a few minutes.
4. Spray the basket of an air fryer with cooking spray.
5. Brush crab patties on both sides with melted butter.
6. Place crab cakes in the air fryer basket and cook at 350 degrees for ten minutes.
7. Turn hamburger patties halfway through cooking.
8. Serve with pleasure.

Sunday Fish With Sticky Sauce

Servings: 2
Cooking: 20 Minutes
Ingredients:

- 1 teaspoon fresh ginger, minced
- 1 teaspoon fresh garlic, minced
- 2 pollack fillets
- Salt and black pepper, to taste

- 1 tablespoon olive oil
- 1 cup chicken broth
- 2 tablespoons light soy sauce
- 1 tablespoon brown sugar
- 2 tablespoons butter, melted
- 2 corn tortillas

Instructions

1. The pollack fillets are patted dry, seasoned with salt and black pepper, and then drizzled with sesame oil.
2. Prepare the fish in the Air Fryer at 380 degrees Fahrenheit for 11 minutes. Slice into bite-sized pieces.
3. In the interim, prepare the sauce. Bring the broth to a boil in a large saucepan. Add soy sauce, sugar, butter, ginger, and garlic to the dish. Reduce the heat to a simmer, and cook until the liquid is somewhat reduced.
4. Add the fish to the heated sauce. Serve on corn tortillas and take pleasure in!

Very Easy Lime-garlic Shrimps

Servings: 1

Cooking: 6 Minutes

Ingredients:

- 1 clove of garlic, minced
- 1 cup raw shrimps
- 1 lime, juiced and zested
- Salt and pepper to taste

Instructions

1. In a mixing bowl, thoroughly toss together all Ingredients.
2. Preheat the air fryer to 3900 degrees Fahrenheit.
3. Insert the shrimp onto the metal skewers that come with the supplementary double-layer rack.
4. Cook for 6 minutes with the rack in place.

Basil Paprika Calamari

Servings: 2
Cooking: 4 Minutes
Ingredients:

- ½ teaspoon white pepper
- 8 oz calamari, peeled, trimmed
- 1 teaspoon ghee, melted
- 1 teaspoon fresh basil, chopped
- ½ teaspoon smoked paprika
- 1 tablespoon apple cider vinegar

Instructions

1. Combine melted ghee, basil, smoked paprika, white pepper, and apple cider vinegar in the shallow bowl. Then, sprinkle the calamari with the ghee mixture and allow it to marinate for a few minutes. Following this, coarsely slice the calamari. Preheat the air fryer to 400 degrees Fahrenheit. Cook the cut calamari for two minutes in an air fryer. Shake the seafood thoroughly and cook for two more minutes.

Butter Paprika Swordfish

Servings: 4
Cooking: 12 Minutes
Ingredients:

- Juice of 1 lemon
- 4 swordfish fillets, boneless
- 1 tablespoon olive oil
- ¾ teaspoon sweet paprika
- 2 teaspoons basil, dried
- 2 tablespoons butter, melted

Instructions

1. Whisk the oil with the remaining ingredients, excluding the fish fillets, in a bowl. Coat the fish with this mixture, set it in the basket of your air fryer, and cook for six minutes on each side. Divide among plates and serve with a salad on the side.

Baby Octopus Hearty Salad

Servings: 3

Cooking: 50 Minutes

Ingredients:

- Salt and pepper to taste
- ¼ cup chopped grilled Halloumi
- 1 long red chili, minced
- 1 ½ tbsp olive oil
- 2 cloves garlic, minced
- 1 ½ tbsp capers
- 1 ¼ tbsp balsamic glaze
- 1 bunch parsley, chopped roughly
- 1 bunch baby fennel, chopped
- 1 cup semi-dried tomatoes, chopped
- 1 red onion, sliced
- A handful of arugula
- 1 ½ cups water

Instructions

1. Pour the water into a pot and bring it to a boil on the stovetop over medium heat. Cut the octopus into bite-sized pieces and place it in the boiling water for 45 seconds; then, drain the water.
2. In a bowl, combine the garlic, olive oil, and octopus. Garnish the octopus with olive oil and garlic. Allow to marinate for a few minutes.
3. Preheat the air fryer to 0 degrees Fahrenheit. Put the octopus in the fryer basket and cook for five minutes. Capers, halloumi, chili, tomatoes, olives, parsley, red onion, fennel, octopus, arugula, and balsamic glaze should be combined in a salad dish. Mix in salt and pepper, then combine. Serve with toasts on the side.

Summer Shrimp Skewers

Servings: 4

Cooking: 15 Minutes + Marinating Time

Ingredients:

- 8 skewers, soaked in water for 30 minutes
- 1 ½ pounds shrimp
- 1/4 cup vermouth
- 2 cloves garlic, crushed
- Kosher salt, to taste
- 1/4 teaspoon black pepper, freshly ground
- 2 tablespoons olive oil
- 1 lemon, cut into wedges

Instructions

1. In a ceramic bowl, combine the shrimp, vermouth, garlic, salt, black pepper, and olive oil; refrigerate for one hour.
2. Remove the shrimp from the marinade and coat them in flour. Thread

onto skewers and place to the cooking basket that has been lightly oiled.

3. Cook at 400 degrees Fahrenheit for 5 minutes, turning once. Serve with wedges of lemon. Bon appétit!

Char-grilled 'n Herbed Sea Scallops

Servings: 3

Cooking: 10 Minutes

Ingredients:

- 1 cup grape tomatoes, halved
- 1-pound sea scallops, meat only
- 3 tablespoons olive oil, divided
- 1 teaspoon dried sage
- Salt and pepper to taste
- 1/3 cup basil leaves, shredded

Instructions

1. Preheat the air fryer to 3900 degrees Fahrenheit.
2. Insert the auxiliary grill pan into the air fryer.
3. Season the scallops with salt, pepper, and half of the olive oil.
4. Place in an air fryer and cook for 10 minutes.
5. Upon completion, serve with tomatoes and basil.
6. Drizzle the remaining olive oil and season to taste with additional salt and pepper.

Herbed Salmon

Servings: 4

Cooking: 15 Minutes

Ingredients:

- ½ teaspoon salt
- 1-pound salmon
- ½ teaspoon dried rosemary
- ½ teaspoon dried thyme
- ½ teaspoon dried basil
- ½ teaspoon ground coriander
- ½ teaspoon ground cumin
- ½ teaspoon ground paprika
- 1 tablespoon olive oil

Instructions

1. Combine rosemary, thyme, basil, coriander, cumin, paprika, and salt in the bowl. Then, massage the salmon lightly with the spice mixture and drizzle with olive oil. Preheat the air fryer to 375 degrees Fahrenheit. Inside the air fryer lined with baking paper, place the prepared fish. Cook the fish for a few minutes, or until a light, crunchy crust forms.

Appetizing Tuna Patties

Servings: 6

Cooking: 10 Minutes

Ingredients:

- 8Salt and black pepper, to taste
- 1 tablespoon fresh lemon juice
- 2 (6-ounce) cans tuna, drained
- ½ cup panko bread crumbs
- 1 egg
- 2 tablespoons fresh parsley, chopped
- 2 teaspoons Dijon mustard
- Dash of Tabasco sauce
- 1 tablespoon olive oil

Instructions

1. Preheat the Air fryer to 355 degrees Fahrenheit and line a baking pan with aluminum foil.
2. All the ingredients should be thoroughly blended in a big bowl.
3. Make patties of equal size from the ingredients and refrigerate them overnight.
4. Place the patties on a baking sheet before transferring them to an Air fryer basket.
5. Cook for approximately 10 minutes and serve warm.

Creamy Breaded Shrimp

Servings: 3
Cooking: 20 Minutes
Ingredients:

- ¼ cup sweet chili sauce
- ¼ cup all-purpose flour
- 1 cup panko breadcrumbs
- 1 pound shrimp, peeled and deveined
- ½ cup mayonnaise
- 1 tablespoon Sriracha sauce

Instructions

1. Prepare an Air fryer basket by greasing it and preheating the Air fryer to 400 degrees Fahrenheit.
2. Flour should be placed in a shallow bowl, while the mayonnaise, chili sauce, and Sriracha sauce should be combined in a separate bowl.
3. Put the breadcrumbs in the last bowl.
4. Coat each shrimp with flour, then dip into the mayonnaise mixture, and then coat with breadcrumbs.

5. Place half of the shrimp in the Air fryer basket and cook for approximately ten minutes.
6. Place the shrimp on serving dishes and repeat with the remaining coating mixture.

Halibut And Capers Mix

Servings: 4

Cooking: 18 Minutes

Ingredients:

- 1 tablespoon lemon juice
- 1 tablespoon olive oil
- 4 halibut fillets, boneless
- A pinch of salt and black pepper
- 1 shallot, chopped
- 2 garlic cloves, minced
- 1 cup parsley, chopped
- 1 tablespoon chives, chopped
- 1 tablespoon lemon zest, grated
- 1 tablespoon capers, drained and chopped
- 1 tablespoon butter, melted

Instructions

1. In a pan that is compatible with your air fryer, heat the oil and butter over medium heat. Add the shallot and garlic and sauté for two minutes. Add the remaining ingredients, excluding the fish, and sauté for an additional three minutes. Add the fish, sear for one minute per side, toss it gently with the herb mixture, set the pan in the air fryer, and cook for 12 minutes at 380 degrees Fahrenheit. To serve, divide everything amongst plates.

Garlic Shrimp Mix

Servings: 3
Cooking: 5 Minutes
Ingredients:

- ½ tablespoon avocado oil
- 1-pound shrimps, peeled
- ½ teaspoon garlic powder
- ¼ teaspoon minced garlic
- 1 teaspoon ground cumin
- ¼ teaspoon lemon zest, grated
- ½ teaspoon dried parsley

Instructions

1. Mix shrimp, garlic powder, minced garlic, cumin, lemon zest, and dry parsley in a mixing bowl. Then, add avocado oil and thoroughly combine the shrimp. Preheat the air fryer to 400 degrees Fahrenheit. Cook the shrimp for five minutes in a preheated air fryer basket.

Great Cat Fish

Servings: 4
Cooking: 25 Minutes
Ingredients:

- ¼ cup seasoned fish fry
- 1 tbsp olive oil
- 1 tbsp parsley, chopped

Instructions

1. Preheat your air fryer to 400 degrees Fahrenheit, then place fillets and seasoned fish fry in a big Ziploc bag; massage well to coat. Place the fillets in the cooking basket of your air fryer and cook for minutes. Flip the fish and continue cooking for 2 to 3 minutes. Serve with parsley on top.

Italian Shrimp

Servings: 4

Cooking: 12 Minutes

Ingredients:

- ½ teaspoon Italian seasoning
- 1 pound shrimp, peeled and deveined
- A pinch of salt and black pepper
- 1 tablespoon sesame seeds, toasted
- 1 tablespoon olive oil

Instructions

1. In a bowl, thoroughly combine the shrimp with the remaining ingredients. Place the shrimp in the basket of the air fryer and cook at 370 degrees Fahrenheit for three minutes.

Potato Casserole Dish

Servings: 4

Cooking: 55 Minutes

Ingredients:

- 1 tsp. cinnamon powder

- 5 tbsp. butter
- 1/4 cup pecans; soaked, drained and ground
- 1/4 cup coconut; shredded
- 3 lbs. sweet potatoes; scrubbed
- 1/4 cup milk
- 2 tbsp. white flour
- 1/4 tsp. allspice; ground
- 1/2 tsp. nutmeg; ground
- Salt to the taste
- For the topping:
- 1/2 cup almond flour
- 1/2 cup walnuts; soaked, drained and ground
- 1/4 cup sugar
- 1 tbsp. chia seeds

Instructions

1. Place potatoes in the basket of your air fryer, puncture them with a fork, and cook at 360 degrees Fahrenheit for 30 minutes.
2. In the meantime, combine together almond flour, pecans, walnuts, 1/4 cup coconut, 1/4 cup sugar, chia seeds, 1 teaspoon of cinnamon, and the butter in a bowl.
3. Transfer potatoes to a cutting board, let them to cool, then peel and set them in an air fryer-compatible baking dish.
4. Stir in the milk, flour, salt, nutmeg, and allspice.
5. Place the dish in the basket of your air fryer and cook it at 400 degrees Fahrenheit for eight minutes. Serve as a side dish by dividing among plates.

Scrambled Eggs

Servings: 2

Cooking: 15 Minutes

Ingredients:

- ½ tsp. coarse salt
- ½ tsp. ground black pepper
- 2 tbsp. olive oil, melted
- 4 eggs, whisked
- 5 oz. fresh spinach, chopped
- 1 medium-sized tomato, chopped
- 1 tsp. fresh lemon juice
- ½ cup of fresh basil, roughly chopped

Instructions

1. Oil the Air Fryer baking pan by tilting it to distribute the oil evenly. Preheat the fryer to 280 degrees Fahrenheit.
2. Mix the remaining ingredients, excluding the basil leaves, thoroughly with a whisk until everything is incorporated.
3. Cook in a fryer for eight to twelve minutes.
4. Before serving, garnish with fresh basil leaves and a dollop of sour cream, if desired.

Simple Cheesy Melty Mushrooms

Servings: 2

Cooking: 20 Minutes

Ingredients:

- 2 cups cheddar cheese, chopped
- Salt and pepper to taste

- 10 button mushromm caps
- 2 cups mozzarella cheese, chopped
- 3 tbsp mixture of Italian herbs

Instructions

1. Preheat your air fryer to 340 degrees Fahrenheit. Combine oil, salt, pepper, and herbs in a bowl to create a marinade. Toss button mushrooms with the marinade to cover thoroughly. In a separate bowl, combine the two cheeses. Cheese mixture to be stuffed into mushrooms. Cook for minutes in the cooking basket of the air fryer.

Mexican-style Cauliflower Fritters

Servings: 6
Cooking: 48 Minutes
Ingredients:

- 1/2 teaspoon crushed red pepper flakes
- 3 eggs, whisked
- 2 teaspoons chili powder
- 1 1/2 teaspoon kosher salt
- 1 teaspoon dried marjoram, crushed
- 2 1/2 cups cauliflower, broken into florets
- 1 1/3 cups tortilla chip crumbs
- 1 ½ cups Queso cotija cheese, crumbled

Instructions

1. Crush the cauliflower florets in a food processor until they are a fine powder (it is the size of rice). Then, combine cauliflower "rice" with the remaining ingredients.
2. Now, shape the cauliflower mixture into small balls and chill for 30

minutes.

3. Set the timer for 14 minutes and preheat the Air Fryer to 5 degrees; cook until the balls are golden and serve immediately.

Lime And Mozzarella Eggplants

Servings: 4

Cooking: 15 Minutes

Ingredients:

- Juice of 1 lime
- 2 tablespoons butter, melted
- 2 tablespoons olive oil
- 2 eggplants, roughly cubed
- 8 ounces mozzarella cheese, shredded
- 3 spring onions, chopped
- 4 eggs, whisked

Instructions

1. In an air fryer-compatible skillet, heat the oil and butter over medium heat. Add the spring onions and eggplants, stir, and cook for 5 minutes. Stir in the eggs and lime juice thoroughly. Sprinkle cheese on top, place the pan in the fryer, and cook at 380 degrees Fahrenheit for several minutes. Serve as a side dish by dividing amongst plates.

Beef Meatballs

Servings: 3

Cooking: 25 Minutes

Ingredients:

- 2 tbsp sugar

- ¼ tsp dry mustard
- 1 small finger ginger, crushed
- 1 tbsp hot sauce
- 3 tbsp vinegar
- 1 ½ tsp lemon juice
- ½ cup tomato ketchup, reduced sugar
- Salt and pepper to taste, if needed

Instructions

1. With a spoon, thoroughly combine the meat, ginger, spicy sauce, vinegar, lemon juice, tomato ketchup, sugar, mustard, pepper, and salt in a bowl. Form two-inch balls with your hands. Do not overcrowd the frying with the balls. Cook at 370 degrees Fahrenheit for minutes while shaking once. Serve alongside tomato dip.

Artichoke Sauté

Servings: 4

Cooking: 10 Minutes

Ingredients:

- 2 teaspoons avocado oil
- 4 artichoke hearts, chopped
- 4 teaspoons lemon juice
- ¼ teaspoon lemon zest, grated

Instructions

1. Preheat the air fryer to 360 degrees Fahrenheit. Sprinkle the chopped artichoke hearts with lemon juice, avocado oil, and lemon zest in the interim. Shake them well and let them marinade for a few minutes. Then, place the artichoke hearts in a hot air fryer and cook for eight

minutes. Shake them vigorously and cook for two more minutes.

Bbq Chicken Pizza

Servings: 1
Cooking: 15 Minutes
Ingredients:

- 2 tbsp red onion, thinly sliced
- ½ chicken herby sausage
- Cooking spray
- ¼ cup barbeque sauce
- ¼ cup shredded mozzarella cheese
- ¼ cup shredded Monterrey Jack cheese
- Chopped cilantro or parsley, for garnish

Instructions

1. Spray the bottom of the naan with cooking spray and place it in the air fryer. Coat the burgers with barbecue sauce, then sprinkle them with mozzarella cheese, Monterrey Jack cheese, and red onion. The crust is topped with sausage and sprayed with cooking spray. Cook for eight minutes at 400 degrees Fahrenheit in a preheated air fryer.

Balsamic Cabbage Mix

Servings: 4
Cooking: 15 Minutes
Ingredients:

- 1 teaspoon lemon juice
- 3 tablespoons olive oil
- 6 cups green cabbage, shredded

- 6 radishes, sliced
- ½ cup celery leaves, chopped
- ¼ cup green onions, chopped
- 2 tablespoons balsamic vinegar
- ½ teaspoon hot paprika

Instructions

1. In the pan of your air fryer, combine all the ingredients and mix them thoroughly.
2. Introduce the pan into the fryer and cook for 15 minutes at 380 degrees Fahrenheit. Serve as a side dish by dividing amongst plates.

Fried Agnolotti

Servings: 6
Cooking: 25 Minutes
Ingredients:

- 2 cups breadcrumbs
- 1 cup flour
- Salt and black pepper
- 4 eggs, beaten
- Cooking spray

Instructions

1. Combine flour, salt, and pepper. First, spaghetti is dipped in flour, then in egg, and finally in breadcrumbs. Spray with oil and arrange in a uniform layer within the air fryer. Cook for minutes at 400 degrees Fahrenheit, rotating once halfway through. Cook till golden brown. Serve goat cheese alongside.

Mung Beans Mix

Servings: 3
Cooking: 16 Minutes
Ingredients:

- 3 tomatoes, chopped
- ½ teaspoon garam masala
- Salt and black pepper to taste
- 1 tablespoon lemon juice
- 1 cup mung beans
- ½ teaspoon olive oil
- 1 teaspoon coriander, ground
- ½ teaspoon turmeric powder
- 1 cup veggie stock
- ½ cup red onion, chopped
- ½ teaspoon cumin seeds
- 4 garlic cloves, minced

Instructions

1. Toss together all of the ingredients in an air fryer-compatible pan.
2. Place the pan in the fryer and cook for 16 minutes at 365 degrees Fahrenheit.
3. The mixture should be divided among plates and served as a side dish.

Rice Pilaf With Cremini Mushrooms

Servings: 6
Cooking: 30 Minutes
Ingredients:

- 2 cups cremini mushrooms, chopped

- Salt and ground black pepper to taste
- 4 cups heated vegetable stock
- 2 cups long-grain rice
- 1 onion, chopped
- 2 garlic cloves, minced
- 1 tbsp fresh chopped parsley, or to taste

Instructions

1. Preheat your air fryer to 400 degrees Fahrenheit.
2. Put a skillet over medium heat. Add rice, oil, onion, and garlic; simmer for five minutes. Whisk together the vegetable stock and mushrooms. season to taste with salt and pepper. Transfer to the basket of your air fryer and cook for several minutes. Garnish with freshly chopped parsley.

Portobello Mushrooms Recipe

Servings: 4

Cooking: 22 Minutes

Ingredients:

- 1 cup almonds; roughly chopped.
- 1 tbsp. parsley
- 1/4 cup olive oil
- 8 cherry tomatoes; halved
- 4 Portobello mushrooms; stems removed and chopped.
- 10 basil leaves
- 1 cup baby spinach
- 3 garlic cloves; chopped
- Salt and black pepper to the taste

Instructions

1. In a food processor, thoroughly combine basil, spinach, garlic, almonds, parsley, oil, salt, black pepper to taste, and mushroom stems.
2. Stuff each mushroom with the mixture, place in an air fryer, and cook at 350 degrees Fahrenheit for one minute. Serve mushrooms on separate dishes.

Turmeric Kale Mix

Servings: 2

Cooking: 12 Minutes

Ingredients:

- ½ cup yellow onion, chopped
- 3 tablespoons butter, melted
- 2 cups kale leaves
- Salt and black pepper to taste
- 2 teaspoons turmeric powder

Instructions

1. Mix all ingredients thoroughly in an air fryer-compatible pan.
2. Place the pan in the fryer and cook for 12 minutes at 0 degrees Fahrenheit.
3. Divide among plates, then serve.

Tomato Bites With Creamy Parmesan Sauce

Servings: 4

Cooking: 20 Minutes

Ingredients:

- For the Sauce:
- 1/2 cup Parmigiano-Reggiano cheese, grated

- 4 tablespoons pecans, chopped
- 1 teaspoon garlic puree
- 1/2 teaspoon fine sea salt
- 1/3 cup extra-virgin olive oil
- For the Tomato Bites:
- 2 large-sized Roma tomatoes, cut into thin slices and pat them dry
- 8 ounces Halloumi cheese, cut into thin slices
- 1/3 cup onions, sliced
- 1 teaspoon dried basil
- 1/4 teaspoon red pepper flakes, crushed
- 1/8 teaspoon sea salt

Instructions

1. Start by heating the Air Fryer to 385 degrees Fahrenheit.
2. In a food processor, combine the sauce ingredients, excluding the extra-virgin olive oil.
3. Slowly and gradually pour in the olive oil while the machine is running; puree until everything is well-combined.
4. Now, apply 1 teaspoon of the sauce to each tomato slice. On each tomato slice, place a slice of Halloumi cheese. Garnish with onion slices. Add basil, red pepper, and salt to taste.
5. Transfer the assembled bites to the cooking basket of an Air Fryer. Cook for approximately 13 minutes after drizzling with nonstick frying spray.
6. Place these bites on a dish and garnish with the remaining sauce before serving at room temperature. Bon appétit!

Grilled Cheese

Servings: 2

Cooking: 25 Minutes

Ingredients:

- 4 slices bread
- ½ cup sharp cheddar cheese
- ¼ cup butter, melted

Instructions

1. Preheat the Air Fryer to 360 degrees Fahrenheit.
2. Place butter and cheese in separate bowls.
3. Brush the butter on each side of the bread slices using a pastry brush.
4. Spread the cheese on two of the bread slices and construct two sandwiches. Place both items in the fryer.
5. Cook for - 7 minutes, or until the cheese is melted and golden brown in color.

Cool Chicken Croquettes

Servings: 4
Cooking: 20 Minutes
Ingredients:

- ½ tsp garlic powder
- 1 egg, beaten
- Salt and pepper to taste
- 1 cup oats, crumbled
- 1 tbsp parsley

Instructions

1. Preheat air fryer to 360 degrees Fahrenheit. Rub garlic, parsley, salt, and pepper into chicken. In a bowl, add beaten egg. In a separate bowl, place oat crumbs. Form croquettes from the chicken mixture and coat them with egg and oats. Put the chicken nuggets in the fryer's basket. Cook for many minutes while shaking once.

Sweet Potato And Chickpea Tacos

Servings: 4

Cooking: 15 Minutes

Ingredients:

- Salt and freshly cracked black pepper, to taste
- 8 corn tortillas
- 1/4 cup Pico de gallo
- 2 cups sweet potato puree
- 2 tablespoons butter, melted
- 14 ounces canned chickpeas, rinsed
- 1 cup Colby cheese, shredded
- 1 teaspoon garlic powder
- 1 teaspoon onion powder
- 2 tablespoons fresh coriander, chopped

Instructions

1. The sweet potatoes should be combined with butter, chickpeas, cheese, garlic powder, onion powder, salt, and black pepper.
2. Spread the sweet potato mixture on each tortilla. 7 minutes at 390 degrees Fahrenheit in a preheated Air Fryer.
3. Decorate with pico de gallo and cilantro. Bon appétit!

Macadamia And Cauliflower Rice

Servings: 4

Cooking: 8 Minutes

Ingredients:

- 1 oz macadamia nuts, grinded
- 9 oz cauliflower

- 1 tablespoon butter
- 3 tablespoons chicken broth

Instructions

1. The cauliflower should be cut into florets. The cauliflower is next grated using the grater. Butter the air fryer pan and place the cauliflower rice inside. Combine ground macadamia nuts with chicken broth. Stir the veggie mixture gently. Cook the cauliflower rice for 8 minutes at 365°F. After 4 minutes of cooking, stir the vegetables.

Smoked Bbq Toasted S

Servings: 1

Cooking: 10 Minutes

Ingredients:

- 1 tsp. chili powder
- ¼ tsp. cumin
- 2 tsp. coconut oil, melted
- ¼ tsp. smoked paprika
- 1 cup raw s

Instructions

1. Mix together the melted coconut oil, paprika, chili powder, and cumin. Place the s in a large dish and equally coat them with coconut oil by pouring it over them and tossing them.
2. Place the s in the fryer's basket and spread them evenly on the bottom.
3. Cook for six minutes at 0 degrees Fahrenheit, occasionally shaking the basket to ensure equal cooking.
4. Allow to cool, then serve.

Crusted Coconut Shrimp

Servings: 5
Cooking: 30 Minutes
Ingredients:

- ⅓ cup cornstarch
- ¾ cup shredded coconut
- 1 tbsp maple syrup
- ½ cup breadcrumbs
- ½ cup milk

Instructions

1. Place the shrimp and cornstarch in a zipper bag and vigorously shake to coat. In a bowl, combine the syrup and milk and leave aside. In a separate bowl, combine the breadcrumbs and coconut shreds. Remove the shrimp from the bag while brushing off any excess flour.
2. The shrimp are first dipped in the milk mixture and then the crumb mixture. Put into the fryer. 1 minute at 350 degrees Fahrenheit, turning once halfway through. Cook to a golden brown color. Serve with a dip made from coconut.

Zucchini And Squash Mix

Servings: 4
Cooking: 12 Minutes
Ingredients:

- 1 teaspoon salt
- 10 oz Kabocha squash
- ½ zucchini, chopped
- 3 spring onions, chopped

- 1 teaspoon dried thyme
- 2 teaspoons ghee
- 1 teaspoon ground turmeric

Instructions

1. Cut the squash into tiny chunks and season with salt and turmeric powder. Add the squash, zucchini, spring onions, dried thyme, and butter to the bowl. Gently shake the vegetables. Preheat the air fryer to 400 degrees Fahrenheit. Cook the vegetable combination for several minutes in an air fryer. Shake the vegetables after six minutes to prevent them from scorching.

Fried Green Beans With Pecorino Romano

Servings: 3
Cooking: 15 Minutes
Ingredients:

- 4 tablespoons Pecorino Romano cheese, finely grated
- Coarse salt and crushed black pepper, to taste
- 1 teaspoon smoked paprika
- 2 tablespoons buttermilk
- 1 egg
- 4 tablespoons cornmeal
- 4 tablespoons tortilla chips, crushed
- 12 ounces green beans, trimmed

Instructions

1. In a shallow bowl, combine the buttermilk and egg using a whisk.
2. Combine the cornmeal, tortilla chips, Pecorino Romano cheese, salt, black pepper, and paprika in a separate bowl.

3. The green beans are dipped in the egg mixture followed by the cornmeal/cheese combination. Place the green beans in the frying basket that has been lightly oiled.
4. Cook for minutes in an Air Fryer preheated to 390 degrees Fahrenheit. Shake the basket and continue cooking for three minutes.
5. Taste, adjust seasonings as necessary, and serve with dipping sauce if preferred. Bon appétit!

Harissa Broccoli Spread

Servings: 4

Cooking: 6 Minutes

Ingredients:

- 1 garlic clove
- 1 teaspoon coconut oil, melted
- 2 cups broccoli, chopped
- 1 teaspoon tahini
- 2 tablespoons sesame oil
- 1 teaspoon salt
- 1 teaspoon harissa

Instructions

1. Preheat the air fryer to 400 degrees Fahrenheit. Place the broccoli and garlic clove in the basket in an air fryer, then drizzle with one teaspoon of sesame oil. The vegetables must cook for six minutes. Then, place the cooked broccoli and garlic in a blender and process until a smooth consistency is achieved. Salt, remaining sesame oil, coconut oil, and harissa should be added. After adding tahini, combine the mixture for a further 30 seconds. Place the prepared hummus in the bowl.

Kale And Sprouts

Servings: 8
Cooking: 15 Minutes
Ingredients:

- Salt and black pepper to the taste
- 1 pound Brussels sprouts, trimmed
- 2 cups kale, torn
- 1 tablespoon olive oil
- 3 ounces mozzarella, shredded

Instructions

1. Except for the mozzarella, mix the remaining ingredients in an air fryer-compatible pan and toss. Place the pan in the air fryer and cook for minutes at 380 degrees Fahrenheit. Distribute among plates, then sprinkle with cheese and serve.

Pumpkin Wedges

Servings: 3
Cooking: 30 Minutes
Ingredients:

- 1 tbsp balsamic vinegar
- Salt and pepper to taste
- 1 tbsp paprika
- 1 whole lime, squeezed
- 1 cup paleo dressing
- 1 tsp turmeric

Instructions

1. Preheat your air fryer to 360 degrees Fahrenheit. Add the pumpkin wedges to the cooking basket of your air fryer and cook for 20 minutes. Mix lime juice, vinegar, turmeric, salt, pepper, and paprika in a bowl to create a marinade. Pour the marinade over the pumpkin and continue cooking for five minutes.

Mint-butter Stuffed Mushrooms

Servings: 3

Cooking: 19 Minutes

Ingredients:

- 1 teaspoon salt, or more to taste
- 1½ tablespoons melted butter
- 3 garlic cloves, minced
- 1 teaspoon ground black pepper, or more to taste
- 1/3 cup seasoned breadcrumbs
- 1½ tablespoons fresh mint, chopped
- 14 medium-sized mushrooms, cleaned, stalks removed

Instructions

1. To prepare the filling, combine all of the aforementioned ingredients, excluding the mushrooms, in a mixing bowl.
2. The mushrooms are then stuffed with the prepared filling.
3. Air-fry filled mushrooms for 12 minutes at 5 degrees Fahrenheit. As an appetizer, check for doneness and serve at room temperature.To prepare the filling, combine all of the aforementioned ingredients, excluding the mushrooms, in a mixing bowl.
4. The mushrooms are then stuffed with the prepared filling.
5. Air-fry filled mushrooms for 12 minutes at 5 degrees Fahrenheit. As an appetizer, check for doneness and serve at room temperature.

Broccoli Patties

Servings: 4
Cooking: 8 Minutes
Ingredients:

- 1 egg, beaten
- ¼ cup coconut flour
- ½ teaspoon onion powder
- 1 cup broccoli, shredded
- ½ teaspoon salt
- ½ teaspoon chili flakes
- 1 teaspoon ground paprika
- 1 teaspoon chives, chopped

Instructions

1. In the mixing bowl, combine onion powder, broccoli shreds, salt, chili flakes, paprika powder, and chives. After incorporating the egg, whisk the mixture with a spoon. Add coconut flour and mix again thoroughly. Create the patties using only your fingertips. Then, prepare the air fryer to 385 degrees Fahrenheit and place the patties within the air fryer basket. Cook them for four minutes per side.

Perfect Crispy Tofu

Servings: 4
Cooking: 20 Minutes
Ingredients:

- 2 tsp sesame oil
- 1 tsp vinegar
- 1 block firm tofu, pressed and cut into 1-inch cubes

- 1 tbsp arrowroot flour
- 2 tbsp soy sauce

Instructions

1. Toss tofu with oil, vinegar, and soy sauce in a bowl and let settle for a few minutes.
2. Toss tofu marinated in arrowroot flour.
3. Spray the basket of an air fryer with cooking spray.
4. Add tofu to the air fryer basket and cook at 370 degrees for 20 minutes. Shake the basket in the middle.
5. Serve with pleasure.

Roasted Almond Delight

Servings: 12
Cooking: 20 Minutes
Ingredients:

- 3 tbsp liquid smoke
- 2 tsp salt
- 2 tbsp molasses

Instructions

1. Preheat your air fryer to 360 degrees Fahrenheit. Add salt, liquid, molasses, and cashews to a bowl and mix to coat. Place in the cooking basket of your air fryer and cook for minutes, shaking the basket every five minutes.

Spiced Green Beans

Servings: 2
Cooking: 10 Minutes
Ingredients:

- 2 tbsp olive oil
- 1/4 tsp ground coriander
- 1/4 tsp ground cumin
- 2 cups green beans
- 1/8 tsp cayenne pepper
- 1/8 tsp ground allspice
- 1/4 tsp ground cinnamon
- 1/2 tsp dried oregano
- 1/2 tsp salt

Instructions

1. Add all items to the big bowl and combine them thoroughly.
2. Spray the basket of an air fryer with cooking spray.
3. Add the bowl's contents to the air fryer basket.
4. 370 Fahrenheit for 10 minutes. Shake the basket halfway
5. Serve with pleasure.

Kabocha Fries

Servings: 2
Cooking: 11 Minutes
Ingredients:

- 6 oz Kabocha squash, peeled
- ½ teaspoon olive oil
- ½ teaspoon salt

Instructions

1. Cut the Kabocha squash into French fry shapes, then drizzle with olive oil. Preheat the air fryer to 390 degrees Fahrenheit. Cook the Kabocha squash fries for five minutes in the air fryer basket. Then, give them a good shake and cook for another 6 minutes. Salt the cooked Kabocha fries and combine thoroughly.

Coconut Parmesan Kale

Servings: 4
Cooking: 15 Minutes
Ingredients:

- 1 and ½ cups coconut cream
- 2 pounds kale, torn
- A pinch of salt and black pepper
- 2 tablespoons olive oil
- 2 garlic cloves, minced
- ½ teaspoon nutmeg, ground
- ½ cup parmesan, grated

Instructions

1. In a pan that fits your air fryer, combine the kale with the remaining ingredients, toss, and cook at 400 degrees Fahrenheit for minutes. Divide among plates, then serve.

Roasted Beet Salad

Servings: 2
Cooking: 20 Minutes + Chilling Time
Ingredients:

- 1/4 teaspoon cumin powder
- Coarse sea salt and ground black pepper, to taste
- 2 medium-sized beets, peeled and cut into wedges
- 2 tablespoons extra virgin olive oil
- 1 tablespoon balsamic vinegar
- 1 teaspoon yellow mustard
- 1 garlic clove, minced
- 1 tablespoon fresh parsley leaves, roughly chopped

Instructions

1. Place the beets in a single layer in the frying basket that has been lightly oiled.
2. 13 minutes at 370 degrees Fahrenheit, while shaking the basket every three minutes.
3. Allow the beets to cool to room temperature before combining them with the remaining ingredients. Serve extremely cold. Enjoy!

Fried Pimiento-stuffed Green Olives

Servings: 4

Cooking: 15 Minutes

Ingredients:

- 1 egg, beaten
- ¼ cup flour
- ¼ cup Parmesan cheese
- Salt and black pepper to taste
- ½ cup panko breadcrumbs
- 1 tsp cayenne pepper

Instructions

1. Preheat the Air fryer to 390 degrees Fahrenheit. Spray the basket of the air fryer with cooking spray.
2. Combine flour, cayenne pepper, salt, and black pepper in a bowl. In another bowl, whisk the egg. In a third bowl, combine panko breadcrumbs with Parmesan cheese.
3. The olives should be drained and dried with a paper towel. Olives are dredged in flour, then egg, and then breadcrumbs. Place in the cooking basket of the air fryer, spray with cooking spray, and cook for 5 minutes before shaking and continuing cooking for an additional minute. Cool the dish before serving.

Low-carb Pita Chips

Servings: 1

Cooking: 15 Minutes

Ingredients:

- ¼ cup blanched finely ground flour
- 1 cup mozzarella cheese, shredded
- 1 egg
- ½ oz. pork rinds, finely ground

Instructions

1. Microwave the mozzarella to melt it. Egg, flour, and pig rinds should be combined to produce a smooth paste. Reheat the cheese if it begins to solidify.
2. Placing the dough between two sheets of parchment paper and flattening it out with a rolling pin to form a rectangle. The thickness is your choice. Cut triangles out of the dough using a sharp knife. This stage may require completion in numerous batches.
3. Place the chips in the fryer for five minutes at 0 degrees Fahrenheit. Flip and heat for an additional five minutes, or until the chips are golden

brown and crisp.

4. Allow the chips to cool and become more rigid. They are suitable for storage in sealed containers.

Cabbage Wedges

Servings: 6

Cooking: 14 Minutes

Ingredients:

- 1 tsp garlic powder
- 1 tsp onion powder
- Pepper
- 1 small cabbage head, cut into wedges
- 3 tbsp olive oil
- 1/4 tsp red chili flakes
- 1/2 tsp fennel seeds
- Salt

Instructions

1. Spray the basket of an air fryer with cooking spray.
2. Combine garlic powder, red chili flakes, fennel seeds, onion powder, pepper, and salt in a small bowl.
3. Coat cabbage wedges with oil, then rub with a mixture of garlic powder and salt.
4. Place cabbage wedges in the air fryer basket and cook for eight minutes at 0 degrees Fahrenheit.
5. Turn cabbage wedges over and cook for a further 6 minutes.
6. Serve with pleasure.

Rainbow Vegetable And Parmesan Croquettes

Servings: 4

Cooking: 40 Minutes

Ingredients:

- 2 eggs
- 1/2 cup panko bread crumbs
- 1 pound potatoes, peeled
- 4 tablespoons milk
- 2 tablespoons butter
- Salt and black pepper, to taste
- 1/2 teaspoon cayenne pepper
- 1/2 cup mushrooms, chopped
- 1/4 cup broccoli, chopped
- 1 carrot, grated
- 1 clove garlic, minced
- 3 tablespoons scallions, minced
- 2 tablespoons olive oil
- 1/2 cup all-purpose flour
- 1/2 cup parmesan cheese, grated

Instructions

1. For twenty minutes, boil the potatoes in a large saucepan. The potatoes are then mashed with milk, butter, salt, black pepper, and cayenne pepper after being drained.
2. Stir together the mushrooms, broccoli, carrots, garlic, scallions, and olive oil. Form the ingredients into patties.
3. In a shallow basin, place the flour; in another bowl, beat the eggs; and in a third bowl, combine the breadcrumbs and parmesan.
4. Coat each patty in flour, then egg, and finally the breadcrumb mixture; press to adhere.

5. Cook at 37 degrees Fahrenheit for 16 minutes in a preheated Air Fryer, shaking halfway during cooking time. Bon appétit!

Kale Mash

Servings: 4
Cooking: 20 Minutes
Ingredients:

- 2 scallions, chopped
- A pinch of salt and black pepper
- 1/3 cup coconut cream
- 1 cauliflower head, florets separated
- 4 teaspoons butter, melted
- 4 garlic cloves, minced
- 3 cups kale, chopped
- 1 tablespoon parsley, chopped

Instructions

1. In an air fryer-compatible pan, combine the cauliflower with the butter, garlic, scallions, salt, pepper, and cream, toss, and then cook at 380 degrees Fahrenheit for 20 minutes. Add the other ingredients, whisk, and divide the mixture across plates.

Sweet Corn Fritters With Avocado

Servings: 3
Cooking: 20 Minutes
Ingredients:

- Sea salt and ground black pepper, to taste
- 1 avocado, peeled, pitted and diced

- 2 cups sweet corn kernels
- 1 small-sized onion, chopped
- 1 garlic clove, minced
- 2 eggs, whisked
- 1 teaspoon baking powder
- 2 tablespoons fresh cilantro, chopped
- 2 tablespoons sweet chili sauce

Instructions

1. Combine the corn, onion, garlic, eggs, baking powder, cilantro, salt, and black pepper in a mixing bowl.
2. Form the corn mixture into six patties and transfer them to the Air Fryer basket that has been lightly oiled.
3. Cook in a preheated Air Fryer at 0 degrees for 8 minutes, then flip and cook for an additional 7 minutes.
4. Serve the fritters with chili sauce and avocado.

Rosemary Olives Mix

Servings: 4

Cooking: 15 Minutes

Ingredients:

- 12 ounces tomatoes, chopped
- 4 garlic cloves, minced
- 2 cups black olives, pitted and halved
- A handful basil, chopped
- 2 rosemary springs, chopped
- 2 red bell peppers, sliced
- 2 tablespoons olive oil

Instructions

1. In an air fryer-compatible pan, combine the olives with the remaining ingredients, toss, and cook at 380 degrees Fahrenheit for minutes. Divide among plates, then serve.

Crispy Wax Beans With Almonds And Blue Cheese

Servings: 3
Cooking: 15 Minutes
Ingredients:

- 1/2 teaspoon red pepper flakes, crushed
- 2 tablespoons almonds, sliced
- 1 pound wax beans, cleaned
- 2 tablespoons peanut oil
- 4 tablespoons seasoned breadcrumbs
- Sea salt and ground black pepper, to taste
- 1/3 cup blue cheese, crumbled

Instructions

1. Toss together the wax beans, peanut oil, breadcrumbs, salt, black pepper, and red pepper.
2. Place the wax beans in the frying basket that has been lightly oiled.
3. Cook for 5 minutes at 400 degrees Fahrenheit in an Air Fryer that has been warmed to temperature. Shake the basket a couple times.
4. Add almonds and heat for a further three minutes, or until gently toasted. Serve with blue cheese over top and enjoy!

Almond Brussels Sprouts

Servings: 4
Cooking: 15 Minutes
Ingredients:

- ½ teaspoon salt
- ½ teaspoon white pepper
- 8 oz Brussels sprouts
- 2 tablespoons almonds, grinded
- 1 teaspoon coconut flakes
- 2 egg whites
- Cooking spray

Instructions

1. Add salt and white pepper to the beaten egg whites. The Brussels sprouts are then split in half and the egg white mixture is added. Coat the vegetables with the ground almonds and coconut flakes after vigorously shaking them. Preheat the air fryer to 380 degrees Fahrenheit. Place the Brussels sprouts in the basket of the air fryer and cook for several minutes. Shake the vegetables after cooking for 8 minutes.

Crumbed Beans

Servings: 4
Cooking: 10 Minutes
Ingredients:

- 2 eggs, beaten
- ½ cup crushed saltines
- ½ cup flour
- 1 tsp. smoky chipotle powder
- ½ tsp. ground black pepper
- 1 tsp. sea salt flakes
- 10 oz. wax beans

Instructions

1. Flour, chipotle powder, black pepper, and salt should be combined in a basin. Place the eggs in another bowl. Place the saltine crackers in a third bowl.
2. Wash the beans in cold water and remove any stringy debris.
3. Before dipping the beans in the beaten egg, coat them with the flour mixture. Finally, cover them with crushed saltine crackers.
4. The beans are sprayed with a frying spray.
5. Air-fry at 360 degrees Fahrenheit for 4 minutes. Shake the cooking basket and continue cooking for three minutes. Serve warm.

Parmesan Asparagus

Servings: 4

Cooking: 5 Minutes

Ingredients:

- 1 tbsp olive oil
- 1/4 tsp pepper
- 1 lb asparagus, cut the ends
- 1/2 cup parmesan cheese, grated
- 1 tbsp fresh lemon juice
- 1 tsp garlic powder
- 1/2 tsp sea salt

Instructions

1. Preheat the air fryer to 390 degrees Fahrenheit.
2. In a large bowl, place asparagus spears.
3. Whisk together olive oil, garlic powder, pepper, and salt in a small basin.
4. Pour the oil mixture over the asparagus and stir thoroughly.
5. Cook the asparagus in the air fryer basket for few minutes.
6. Sprinkle grated cheese over cooked asparagus and drizzle with lemon juice.

7. Serve with pleasure.

Creamy Broccoli And Cauliflower

Servings: 4
Cooking: 20 Minutes
Ingredients:

- 2 tablespoons mustard
- 1 cup sour cream
- 15 ounces broccoli florets
- 10 ounces cauliflower florets
- 1 leek, chopped
- 2 spring onions, chopped
- Salt and black pepper to the taste
- 2 ounces butter, melted
- 5 ounces mozzarella cheese, shredded

Instructions

1. In a baking dish that is compatible with an air fryer, spread the butter evenly. Toss together the broccoli, cauliflower, and the remaining ingredients, excluding the mozzarella. Then, place the pan in the air fryer and cook at 380 degrees Fahrenheit for twenty minutes. Serve as a side dish by dividing amongst plates.

Fennel With Shirataki Noodles

Servings: 3
Cooking: 20 Minutes + Chilling Time
Ingredients:

- 1 teaspoon ginger, freshly grated

- 1 tablespoon soy sauce
- 1 fennel bulb, quartered
- Salt and white pepper, to taste
- 1 clove garlic, finely chopped
- 1 green onion, thinly sliced
- 1 cup Chinese cabbage, shredded
- 2 tablespoons rice wine vinegar
- 2 tablespoons sesame oil
- 1 1/3 cups Shirataki noodles, boiled

Instructions

1. Begin by heating the Air Fryer to 370 degrees Fahrenheit.
2. Now, cook the fennel bulb in the lightly oiled cooking basket for 15 minutes while shaking the basket every so often.
3. Allow it to cool completely before combining it with the remaining ingredients. Serve extremely cold.

Cranberry Beans Side Salad

Servings: 6

Cooking: 15 Minutes

Ingredients:

- Salt and black pepper to taste
- 25 ounces canned tomatoes, drained and chopped
- 6 garlic cloves, minced
- 2½ cups canned cranberry beans, drained
- 1 yellow onion, chopped
- 2 celery ribs, chopped
- ½ teaspoon smoked paprika
- ½ teaspoon red pepper flakes
- 3 teaspoons basil, chopped

- 10 ounces kale, torn

Instructions

1. In a pan that is compatible with your air fryer, combine all of the ingredients.
2. Cook the pan at 370 degrees Fahrenheit for fifteen minutes.
3. Divide across plates and serve as a side salad.

Greek-style Roasted Tomatoes With Feta

Servings: 2
Cooking: 20 Minutes
Ingredients:

- 1/2 teaspoon sea salt
- 3 medium-sized tomatoes, cut into four slices, pat dry
- 1 teaspoon dried basil
- 1 teaspoon dried oregano
- 1/4 teaspoon red pepper flakes, crushed
- 3 slices Feta cheese

Instructions

1. The tomatoes are sprayed with cooking oil and transferred to the Air Fryer basket. Utilize various seasonings.
2. Cook at 350 degrees Fahrenheit for approximately 8 minutes, rotating halfway through.
3. Add cheese and simmer for an additional 4 minutes. Bon appétit!

American-style Brussel Sprout Salad

Servings: 4

Cooking: 35 Minutes

Ingredients:

- 1 small-sized red onion, chopped
- 1 pound Brussels sprouts
- 1 apple, cored and diced
- 1/2 cup mozzarella cheese, crumbled
- 1/2 cup pomegranate seeds
- 4 eggs, hardboiled and sliced
- Dressing:
- 1/4 cup olive oil
- 2 tablespoons champagne vinegar
- 1 teaspoon Dijon mustard
- 1 teaspoon honey
- Sea salt and ground black pepper, to taste

Instructions

1. Begin by heating the Air Fryer to 380 degrees Fahrenheit.
2. The Brussels sprouts should be added to the cooking basket. Cook for 15 minutes after sprinkling with cooking spray and heating for the same amount of time. Allow it to reach room temperature in roughly 15 minutes.
3. The Brussels sprouts should be combined with the apple, cheese, pomegranate seeds, and red onion.
4. Toss together all ingredients for the dressing and blend thoroughly. Serve with the hard-boiled eggs on top. Bon appétit!

Crispy Parmesan Asparagus

Servings: 4

Cooking: 20 Minutes

Ingredients:

- 1 cup bread crumbs
- Sea salt and ground black pepper, to taste
- 2 eggs
- 1 teaspoon Dijon mustard
- 1 cup Parmesan cheese, grated
- 18 asparagus spears, trimmed
- 1/2 cup sour cream

Instructions

1. Begin by heating the Air Fryer to 400 degrees Fahrenheit.
2. In a shallow bowl, combine the eggs and mustard using a whisk. Combine the Parmesan cheese, breadcrumbs, salt, and black pepper in another shallow bowl.
3. Coat the asparagus stalks in the egg mixture, then press them into the parmesan mixture.
4. Cook for five minutes and in three separate batches. Serve with a side of sour cream. Enjoy!

Roasted Vegetables

Servings: 6

Cooking: 30 Minutes

Ingredients:

- 1 tbsp. fresh thyme needles
- 1 ⅓ cup small parsnips

- 1 ⅓ cup celery [3 – 4 stalks]
- 2 red onions
- 1 ⅓ cup small butternut squash
- 1 tbsp. olive oil
- Salt and pepper to taste

Instructions

1. Pre-heat the Air Fryer to 390 degrees Fahrenheit.
2. The parsnips and onions are peeled and cut into cm cubes. Onions are cut into wedges.
3. Not necessary to peel the butternut squash. Cut it in half, remove the seeds, and cube it.
4. Combine the thyme, olive oil, salt, and pepper with the chopped vegetables.
5. Transfer the basket containing the veggies to the Air Fryer.
6. Cook for 20 minutes, stirring once throughout cooking, until the vegetables are evenly browned and fully cooked.

Sweet Corn Fritters

Servings: 4
Cooking: 20 Minutes
Ingredients:

- 2 tbsp. plain milk
- 1 cup of Parmesan cheese, grated
- ¼ cup flour
- ⅓ tsp. baking powder
- 1 medium-sized carrot, grated
- 1 yellow onion, finely chopped
- 4 oz. canned sweet corn kernels, drained
- 1 tsp. sea salt flakes

- 1 heaping tbsp. fresh cilantro, chopped
- 1 medium-sized egg, whisked
- ⅓ tsp. sugar

Instructions

1. Place the grated carrot in a sieve and squeeze it to remove excess liquid. It was dried using a paper towel.
2. Carrots should be combined with the remaining ingredients.
3. Form one tablespoon of the ingredients into a ball and flatten it with your palm or a spoon. Repeat until the remaining mixture is consumed.
4. The balls should be sprayed with cooking spray.
5. Place the balls in the Air Fryer's basket without overlapping them. Cook at 3°F for eight to eleven minutes, or until firm.
6. Serve hot.

Fried Asparagus With Goat Cheese

Servings: 3

Cooking: 15 Minutes

Ingredients:

- 1/4 teaspoon cracked black pepper, to taste
- 1/2 teaspoon dried dill weed
- 1 bunch of asparagus, trimmed
- 1 tablespoon olive oil
- 1/2 teaspoon kosher salt
- 1/2 cup goat cheese, crumbled

Instructions

1. Place the asparagus spears in the cooking basket that has been lightly oiled. Combine the olive oil, salt, black pepper, and dill with the

asparagus.

2. 9 minutes at 400 degrees Fahrenheit in a preheated Air Fryer.
3. Serve goat cheese as a garnish. Bon appétit!

Mushroom Cakes

Servings: 4

Cooking: 8 Minutes

Ingredients:

- 1 teaspoon dried parsley
- ½ teaspoon ground black pepper
- 1 teaspoon sesame oil
- 9 oz mushrooms, finely chopped
- ¼ cup coconut flour
- 1 teaspoon salt
- 1 egg, beaten
- 3 oz Cheddar cheese, shredded
- 1 oz spring onion, chopped

Instructions

1. Mix chopped mushrooms, coconut flour, salt, egg, dried parsley, ground black pepper, and minced onion in a mixing dish. Stir the mixture until it is smooth, then stir in the Cheddar cheese. With the help of a fork, stir it. Preheat the air fryer to 385 degrees Fahrenheit. Line the pan of the air fryer with baking paper. Create medium-sized patties with the spoon and place them in the pan. The patties are seasoned with sesame oil and cooked for four minutes per side.

Simple Green Beans With Butter

Servings: 4

Cooking: 12 Minutes

Ingredients:

- 1/2 teaspoon mixed peppercorns, freshly cracked
- 1 tablespoon butter
- 3/4 pound green beans, cleaned
- 1 tablespoon balsamic vinegar
- 1/4 teaspoon kosher salt
- 2 tablespoons toasted sesame seeds, to serve

Instructions

1. Set your Air Fryer to 390 degrees Fahrenheit.
2. Except for the sesame seeds, combine the green beans with all of the ingredients listed above, excluding the sesame seeds. Adjust the timer to ten minutes.
3. In the meantime, toast the sesame seeds in a small nonstick skillet, stirring constantly.
4. Serve sautéed green beans with toasted sesame seeds on a beautiful serving dish. Bon appétit!

Dill Corn

Servings: 4

Cooking: 6 Minutes

Ingredients:

- 2 tablespoons butter, melted
- 4 ears of corn
- Salt and black pepper to taste

- 2 tablespoon dill, chopped

Instructions

1. Combine the salt, pepper, and butter in a bowl.
2. After coating the corn with the butter mixture, place it in the air fryer.
3. Six minutes at 0 degrees Fahrenheit.
4. Place the corn on individual plates, then sprinkle the dill on top.

Smoked Asparagus

Servings: 4
Cooking: 20 Minutes
Ingredients:

- 1 tablespoon smoked paprika
- 1 pound asparagus stalks
- Salt and black pepper to the taste
- ¼ cup olive oil+ 1 teaspoon
- 2 tablespoons balsamic vinegar
- 1 tablespoon lime juice

Instructions

1. In a bowl, combine the asparagus, salt, pepper, and 1 teaspoon of oil; toss, then add to the basket of the air fryer and cook at 370 degrees Fahrenheit for 20 minutes. Meanwhile, whisk together the remaining ingredients in a bowl. As a side dish, divide the asparagus into plates and drizzle with balsamic vinaigrette.

Greek-style Vegetable Bake

Servings: 4

Cooking: 35 Minutes

Ingredients:

- 1 teaspoon dried oregano
- 1 teaspoon smoked paprika
- Salt and ground black pepper, to taste
- 1 tomato, sliced
- 1 eggplant, peeled and sliced
- 2 bell peppers, seeded and sliced
- 1 red onion, sliced
- 1 teaspoon fresh garlic, minced
- 4 tablespoons olive oil
- 1 teaspoon mustard
- 6 ounces halloumi cheese, sliced lengthways

Instructions

1. Begin by heating the Air Fryer to 370 degrees Fahrenheit. Spray a baking dish with cooking spray that prevents sticking.
2. Place the eggplant, peppers, onion, and garlic in the baking dish's bottom. Add olive oil, mustard, and spices to the dish. Cook for 14 minutes after transfer to the cooking basket.
3. Increase the temperature to 0 degrees Fahrenheit and cook for an additional 5 minutes until bubbling. Before serving, allow it to rest for 10 minutes on a cooling rack.
4. Bon appétit!

Coconut Mushrooms Mix

Servings: 4

Cooking: 15 Minutes

Ingredients:

- Salt and black pepper to the taste
- 2 tablespoons olive oil
- 1 pound brown mushrooms, sliced
- 1 pound kale, torn
- 14 ounces coconut milk

Instructions

1. In an air fryer-compatible skillet, combine the kale with the remaining ingredients and stir. Place the pan in the fryer and cook at 380 degrees Fahrenheit for a few minutes.

5

VEGETABLE & SIDE DISHES

Air Fried Halloumi With Veggies

Servings: 2
Cooking: 15 Minutes
Ingredients:

- 2 zucchinis, cut into even chunks
- 1 large carrot, cut into chunks
- 1 large eggplant, peeled, cut into chunks
- 2 tsp olive oil
- 1 tsp dried mixed herbs
- Salt and black pepper

Instructions

1. In a bowl, add halloumi, zucchini, carrot, eggplant, olive oil, herbs, salt, and pepper. Sprinkle with oil, salt, and pepper. Arrange halloumi and veggies on the air fryer basket and drizzle with olive oil. Cook for minutes at 340 F, shaking once. Sprinkle with mixed herbs to serve.

Delicious Asparagus And Mushroom Fritters

Servings: 4

Cooking: 15 Minutes

Ingredients:

- 1 pound asparagus spears
- 1 tablespoon canola oil
- 1 teaspoon paprika
- Sea salt and freshly ground black pepper, to taste
- 1 teaspoon garlic powder
- 3 tablespoons scallions, chopped
- 1 cup button mushrooms, chopped
- 1/2 cup fresh breadcrumbs
- 1 tablespoon flax seeds, soaked in 2 tablespoons of water
- 4 tablespoons sun-dried tomato hummus

Instructions

1. Place the asparagus spears in the lightly greased cooking basket. Toss the asparagus with the canola oil, paprika, salt, and black pepper.
2. Cook in the preheated Air Fryer at 400 degrees F for 5 minutes. Chop the asparagus spears and add the garlic powder, scallions, mushrooms, breadcrumbs, and vegan "egg".
3. Mix until everything is well incorporated and form the asparagus mixture into patties.
4. Cook in the preheated Air Fryer at 0 degrees F for 5 minutes, flipping halfway through the cooking time. Serve with sun-dried tomato hummus. Bon appétit!

Minty Green Beans With Shallots

Servings: 6

Cooking: 25 Minutes

Ingredients:

- 1 tablespoon fresh mint, chopped
- 1 tablespoon sesame seeds, toasted
- 1 tablespoon vegetable oil
- 1 teaspoon soy sauce
- 1-pound fresh green beans, trimmed
- 2 large shallots, sliced
- 2 tablespoons fresh basil, chopped
- 2 tablespoons pine nuts

Instructions

1. Preheat the air fryer to 3300F.
2. Place the grill pan accessory in the air fryer.
3. In a mixing bowl, combine the green beans, shallots, vegetable oil, and soy sauce.
4. Dump in the air fryer and cook for 25 minutes.
5. Once cooked, garnish with basil, mints, sesame seeds, and pine nuts.

Layered Tortilla Bake

Servings: 6

Cooking: 30 Minutes

Ingredients:

- 1 (15 ounce) can black beans, rinsed and drained
- 1 cup salsa
- 1 cup salsa, divided

- 1/2 cup chopped tomatoes
- 1/2 cup sour cream
- 2 (15 ounce) cans pinto beans, drained and rinsed
- 2 cloves garlic, minced
- 2 cups shredded reduced-fat Cheddar cheese
- 2 tablespoons chopped fresh cilantro
- 7 (8 inch) flour tortillas

Instructions

1. Mash pinto beans in a large bowl and mix in garlic and salsa.
2. In another bowl whisk together tomatoes, black beans, cilantro, and ¼ cup salsa.
3. Lightly grease baking pan of air fryer with cooking spray. Spread 1 tortilla, spread ¾ cup pinto bean mixture evenly up to ½-inch away from the edge of tortilla, spread ¼ cup cheese on top. Cover with another tortilla, spread 2/cup black bean mixture, and then ¼ cup cheese. Repeat twice the layering process. Cover with the last tortilla, top with pinto bean mixture and then cheese.
4. Cover pan with foil.
5. Cook for 2minutes at 390oF, remove foil and cook for 5 minutes or until tops are lightly browned.
6. Serve and enjoy.

Refreshingly Zesty Broccoli

Servings: 4

Cooking: 15 Minutes

Ingredients:

- 1 tablespoon butter
- 1 large head broccoli, cut into bite-sized pieces
- 1 tablespoon white sesame seeds

- 2 tablespoons vegetable stock
- 1 tablespoon fresh lemon juice
- 3 garlic cloves, chopped
- ½ teaspoon fresh lemon zest, grated finely
- ½ teaspoon red pepper flakes, crushed

Instructions

1. Preheat the Air fryer to 355 o F and grease an Air fryer pan.
2. Mix butter, vegetable stock and lemon juice in the Air fryer pan.
3. Transfer into the Air fryer and cook for about 2 minutes.
4. Stir in garlic and broccoli and cook for about 1minutes.
5. Add sesame seeds, lemon zest and red pepper flakes and cook for minutes.
6. Dish out and serve warm.

Air-fried Cauliflower

Servings: 4

Cooking: 20 Minutes

Ingredients:

- 2 tbsp olive oil
- ½ tsp salt
- ¼ tsp freshly ground black pepper

Instructions

1. In a bowl, toss cauliflower, oil, salt, and black pepper, until the florets are well-coated. Arrange the florets in the air fryer and cook for 8 minutes at 360 F; work in batches if needed. Serve the crispy cauliflower in lettuce wraps with chicken, cheese or mushrooms.

Veggie Fingers With Monterey Jack Cheese

Servings: 4
Cooking: 20 Minutes
Ingredients:

- 10 ounces cauliflower
- 1/4 cup almond flour
- 1 ½ teaspoons soy sauce
- Salt and freshly ground black pepper, to taste
- 1 teaspoon cayenne pepper
- 1 cup parmesan cheese, grated
- 3/4 teaspoon dried dill weed
- 1 tablespoon olive oil

Instructions

1. Firstly, pulse the cauliflower in your food processor; transfer them to a bowl and add 4 cup almond flour, soy sauce, salt, black pepper, and cayenne pepper.
2. Roll the mixture into veggie fingers shape. In another bowl, place grated parmesan cheese and dried dill.
3. Now, coat the veggie fingers with the parmesan mixture, covering completely. Drizzle veggie fingers with olive oil.
4. Air-fry for 15 minutes at 350 degrees F; turn them over once or twice during the cooking time. Eat with your favorite sauce. Enjoy!

Marinated Tofu Bowl With Pearl Onions

Servings: 4
Cooking: 1 Hour 20 Minutes
Ingredients:

- 16 ounces firm tofu, pressed and cut into 1-inch pieces
- 2 tablespoons vegan Worcestershire sauce
- 1 tablespoon apple cider vinegar
- 1 tablespoon maple syrup
- 1/2 teaspoon shallot powder
- 1/2 teaspoon porcini powder
- 1/2 teaspoon garlic powder
- 2 tablespoons peanut oil
- 1 cup pearl onions, peeled

Instructions

1. Place the tofu, Worcestershire sauce, vinegar, maple syrup, shallot powder, porcini powder, and garlic powder in a ceramic dish. Let it marinate in your refrigerator for hour.
2. Transfer the tofu to the lightly greased Air Fryer basket. Add the peanut oil and pearl onions; toss to combine.
3. Cook the tofu with the pearl onions in the preheated Air Fryer at 0 degrees F for 6 minutes; pause and brush with the reserved marinade; cook for a further 5 minutes.
4. Serve immediately. Bon appétit!

Tofu In Sweet & Sour Sauce

Servings: 3
Cooking: 25 Minutes
Ingredients:

- 2 tablespoons Shoyu sauce
- 16 ounces extra-firm tofu, drained, pressed and cubed
- 1/2 cup water
- 1/4 cup pineapple juice
- 2 garlic cloves, minced

- 1/2 teaspoon fresh ginger, grated
- 1 teaspoon cayenne pepper
- 1/4 teaspoon ground black pepper
- 1/2 teaspoon salt
- 1 teaspoon honey
- 1 tablespoon arrowroot powder

Instructions

1. Drizzle the Shoyu sauce all over the tofu cubes. Cook in the preheated Air Fryer at 380 degrees F for 6 minutes; shake the basket and cook for a further 5 minutes.
2. Meanwhile, cook the remaining ingredients in a heavy skillet over medium heat for 10 minutes, until the sauce has slightly thickened.
3. Stir the fried tofu into the sauce and continue cooking for 4 minutes more or until the tofu is thoroughly heated.
4. Serve warm and enjoy!

Oatmeal Stuffed Bell Peppers

Servings: 2

Cooking: 16 Minutes

Ingredients:

- 2 large red bell peppers, halved lengthwise and seeded
- 2 cups cooked oatmeal
- 4 tablespoons canned red kidney beans, rinsed and drained
- 4 tablespoons coconut yogurt
- ¼ teaspoon ground cumin
- ¼ teaspoon smoked paprika
- Salt and ground black pepper, as required

Instructions

1. Set the temperature of air fryer to 355 degrees F. Grease an air fryer basket.
2. Arrange bell peppers into the prepared air fryer basket, cut-side down.
3. Air fry for about 8 minutes.
4. Remove from the air fryer and set aside to cool.
5. Meanwhile, in a bowl, mix well oatmeal, beans, coconut yogurt, and spices.
6. Stuff each bell pepper half with the oatmeal mixture.
7. Now, set the air fryer to 355 degrees F.
8. Arrange bell peppers into the air fryer basket and air fry for about minutes.
9. Remove from air fryer and transfer the bell peppers onto a serving platter.
10. Set aside to cool slightly.
11. Serve warm.

Grilled 'n Glazed Strawberries

Servings: 2

Cooking: 20 Minutes

Ingredients:

- 1 tbsp honey
- 1 tsp lemon zest
- 1-lb large strawberries
- 3 tbsp melted butter
- Lemon wedges
- Pinch kosher salt

Instructions

1. Thread strawberries in 4 skewers.
2. In a small bowl, mix well remaining Ingredients except for lemon

wedges. Brush all over strawberries.
3. Place skewer on air fryer skewer rack.
4. For 10 minutes, cook on 360oF. Halfway through cooking time, brush with honey mixture and turnover skewer.
5. Serve and enjoy with a squeeze of lemon.

Eggplant Caviar

Servings: 3
Cooking: 20 Minutes
Ingredients:

- ½ red onion, chopped and blended
- 2 tbsp balsamic vinegar
- 1 tbsp olive oil
- salt

Instructions

1. Arrange the eggplants in the basket and cook them for minutes at 380 F. Remove them and let them cool. Then cut the eggplants in half, lengthwise, and empty their insides with a spoon.
2. Blend the onion in a blender. Put the inside of the eggplants in the blender and process everything. Add the vinegar, olive oil and salt, then blend again. Serve cool with bread and tomato sauce or ketchup.

Sweet And Sour Brussel Sprouts

Servings: 2
Cooking: 10 Minutes
Ingredients:

- 2 cups Brussels sprouts, trimmed and halved lengthwise

- 1 tablespoon balsamic vinegar
- 1 tablespoon maple syrup
- Salt, as required

Instructions

1. Preheat the Air fryer to 400 o F and grease an Air fryer basket.
2. Mix all the ingredients in a bowl and toss to coat well.
3. Arrange the Brussel sprouts in the Air fryer basket and cook for about 10 minutes, shaking once halfway through.
4. Dish out in a bowl and serve hot.

Asian-style Cauliflower

Servings: 4
Cooking: 25 Minutes
Ingredients:

- 2 cups cauliflower, grated
- 1 onion, peeled and finely chopped
- 1 tablespoon sesame oil
- 1 tablespoon tamari sauce
- 1 tablespoon sake
- 2 cloves garlic, peeled and pressed
- 1 tablespoon ginger, freshly grated
- 1 tablespoon fresh parsley, finely chopped
- 1/4 cup of lime juice
- 2 tablespoons sesame seeds

Instructions

1. Combine the cauliflower, onion, sesame oil, tamari sauce, sake, garlic, and the ginger in a mixing dish; stir until everything's well incorporated.

2. Air-fry at 400 degrees F for 1minutes.
3. Pause the Air Fryer. Add the parsley and lemon juice. Turn the machine to cook at 0 degrees F; cook additional 10 minutes.
4. Meanwhile, toast the sesame seeds in a non-stick skillet; stir them constantly over a medium-low flame. Sprinkle over prepared cauliflower and serve warm.

Shallots 'n Almonds On French Green Beans

Servings: 4

Cooking: 10 Minutes

Ingredients:

- ¼ cup slivered almonds, toasted
- ½ pounds shallots, peeled and cut into quarters
- ½ teaspoon ground white pepper
- 1 ½ pound French green beans, stems removed and blanched
- 1 tablespoon salt
- 2 tablespoon olive oil

Instructions

1. Preheat the air fryer to 4000F.
2. Mix all ingredients in a mixing bowl. Toss until well combined.
3. Place inside the air fryer basket and cook for 10 minutes or until lightly browned.

Rosemary Au Gratin Potatoes

Servings: 4

Cooking: 45 Minutes

Ingredients:

- 2 pounds potatoes
- 1/4 cup sunflower kernels, soaked overnight
- 1/2 cup almonds, soaked overnight
- 1 cup unsweetened almond milk
- 2 tablespoons nutritional yeast
- 1 teaspoon shallot powder
- 2 fresh garlic cloves, minced
- 1/2 cup water
- Kosher salt and ground black pepper, to taste
- 1 teaspoon cayenne pepper
- 1 tablespoon fresh rosemary

Instructions

1. Bring a large pan of water to a boil. Cook the whole potatoes for about 20 minutes. Drain the potatoes and let sit until cool enough to handle.
2. Peel your potatoes and slice into 1/8-inch rounds.
3. Add the sunflower kernels, almonds, almond milk, nutritional yeast, shallot powder, and garlic to your food processor; blend until uniform, smooth, and creamy. Add the water and blend for seconds more.
4. Place 1/2 of the potatoes overlapping in a single layer in the lightly greased casserole dish. Spoon 1/2 of the sauce on top of the potatoes. Repeat the layers, ending with the sauce.
5. Top with salt, black pepper, cayenne pepper, and fresh rosemary. Bake in the preheated Air Fryer at 32degrees F for 20 minutes. Serve warm.

Creole Seasoned Vegetables

Servings: 5
Cooking: 15 Minutes
Ingredients:

- ¼ cup honey

- ¼ cup yellow mustard
- 1 large red bell pepper, sliced
- 1 teaspoon black pepper
- 1 teaspoon salt
- 2 large yellow squash, cut into ½ inch thick slices
- 2 medium zucchinis, cut into ½ inch thick slices
- 2 teaspoons creole seasoning
- 2 teaspoons smoked paprika
- 3 tablespoons olive oil

Instructions

1. Preheat the air fryer to 3300F.
2. Place the grill pan accessory in the air fryer.
3. In a Ziploc bag, put the zucchini, squash, red bell pepper, olive oil, salt and pepper. Give a shake to season all vegetables.
4. Place on the grill pan and cook for 15 minutes.
5. Meanwhile, prepare the sauce by combining the mustard, honey, paprika, and creole seasoning. Season with salt to taste.
6. Serve the vegetables with the sauce.

Tomato Sandwiches With Feta And Pesto

Servings: 2

Cooking: 60 Minutes

Ingredients:

- 1 (4- oz) block Feta cheese
- 1 small red onion, thinly sliced
- 1 clove garlic
- Salt to taste
- 2 tsp + ¼ cup olive oil
- 1 ½ tbsp toasted pine nuts

- ¼ cup chopped parsley
- ¼ cup grated Parmesan cheese
- ¼ cup chopped basil

Instructions

1. Add basil, pine nuts, garlic and salt to a food processor. Process while adding the ¼ cup of olive oil slowly. Once the oil is finished, pour the basil pesto into a bowl and refrigerate for 30 minutes.
2. Preheat the air fryer to 390 F. Slice the feta cheese and tomato into ½ inch circular slices. Use a kitchen towel to pat the tomatoes dry. Remove the pesto from the fridge and use a tablespoon to spread some pesto on each slice of tomato. Top with a slice of feta cheese. Add the onion and remaining olive oil in a bowl and toss. Spoon on top of feta cheese.
3. Place the tomato in the fryer's basket and cook for 12 minutes. Remove to a serving platter, sprinkle lightly with salt and top with the remaining pesto. Serve with a side of rice or lean meat.

Oatmeal Stuffed Bell Pepper

Servings: 2
Cooking: 16 Minutes
Ingredients:

- 1 large red bell pepper, halved and seeded
- 1 cup cooked oatmeal
- 2 tablespoons canned red kidney beans
- 2 tablespoons plain yogurt
- 1/8 teaspoon ground cumin
- 1/8 teaspoon smoked paprika
- Salt and black pepper, to taste

Instructions

1. Prepare the air fryer by preheating it to 355 degrees Fahrenheit and greasing the air fryer pan.
2. Place the red bell peppers in the pan for the air fryer and cook for approximately 8 minutes.
3. In the meantime, combine the remaining ingredients with the oats in a bowl.
4. Cook the peppers for approximately 8 minutes after stuffing each half with the oatmeal mixture.
5. Place in a bowl and serve at a warm temperature.

Hearty Carrots

Servings: 4

Cooking: 25 Minutes

Ingredients:

- ¼ cup yogurt
- 2 garlic cloves, minced
- 2 shallots, chopped
- 3 carrots, sliced
- Salt to taste
- 3 tbsp parsley, chopped

Instructions

1. Preheat the air fryer to 370 degrees Fahrenheit. Combine the carrots, salt, garlic, shallots, parsley, and yogurt in a bowl and mix well. Oil should be sprinkled on top. Put the vegetables in the basket of the air fryer, and let them cook for a few minutes. Garnish with basil and garlic mayonnaise before serving.

Barbecue Tofu With Green Beans

Servings: 3

Cooking: 1 Hour

Ingredients:

- 1/4 teaspoon smoked paprika
- 1/2 teaspoon freshly grated ginger
- 2 cloves garlic, minced
- 12 ounces super firm tofu, pressed and cubed
- 1/4 cup ketchup
- 1 tablespoon white vinegar
- 1 tablespoon coconut sugar
- 1 tablespoon mustard
- 1/4 teaspoon ground black pepper
- 1/2 teaspoon sea salt
- 2 tablespoons olive oil
- 1 pound green beans

Instructions

1. Toss the tofu in the mixture consisting of ketchup, white vinegar, coconut sugar, mustard, black pepper, smoked paprika, sea salt, ginger, and garlic, along with the olive oil. Let it marinade for 30 minutes.
2. Cook at a temperature of 360 degrees Fahrenheit for ten minutes, then flip them over and continue cooking for an additional minute. Reserve.
3. Put the green beans in the basket of the air fryer and lightly coat it in butter. Roast for five minutes at 400 degrees Fahrenheit. Bon appétit!

Spicy Veggie Recipe From Thailand

Servings: 4

Cooking: 15 Minutes

Ingredients:

- 2 pounds vegetable of your choice, sliced into cubes
- 2 tablespoons fish sauce
- 1 ½ cups packed cilantro leaves
- 1 tablespoon black pepper
- 1 tablespoon chili garlic sauce
- 1/3 cup vegetable oil
- 8 cloves of garlic, minced

Instructions

1. Preheat the air fryer to 3300 degrees Fahrenheit.
2. The grill pan attachment should be placed inside the air fryer.
3. Put all of the ingredients into the mixing bowl and give it a good toss so that everything is evenly coated.
4. Place in the grill pan, and let it cook for fifteen minutes.

The Best Falafel Ever

Servings: 2

Cooking: 20 Minutes

Ingredients:

- 1 teaspoon cumin powder
- A pinch of ground cardamom
- 1 cup dried chickpeas, soaked overnight
- 1 small-sized onion, chopped
- 2 cloves garlic, minced

- 2 tablespoons fresh cilantro leaves, chopped
- 1 tablespoon flour
- 1/2 teaspoon baking powder
- Sea salt and ground black pepper, to taste

Instructions

1. In a food processor, blitz all of the ingredients together until the chickpeas are completely ground.
2. Make the falafel mixture into balls, then set them in the basket of the air fryer that has been greased lightly.
3. Cook for approximately 15 minutes at a temperature of 0 degrees Fahrenheit, shaking the basket occasionally to achieve equal cooking.
4. Place each portion in a pita pocket and top with the toppings of your choosing. Enjoy!

Kid-friendly Zucchini Fries

Servings: 4

Cooking: 20 Minutes

Ingredients:

- 1/2 teaspoon shallot powder
- 1/3 teaspoon freshly ground black pepper, or more to taste
- 2 tablespoons olive oil
- 1/2 teaspoon smoked cayenne pepper
- 1 large zucchini, peeled and cut into 1/4-inch long slices
- 3/4 teaspoon garlic salt

Instructions

1. To begin, set the temperature on your Air Fryer to 360 degrees Fahrenheit.

2. The next step is to place the zucchini in a mixing dish and combine it with the remaining ingredients.
3. About 14 minutes should be enough time to cook the zucchini fries. You can serve these with whatever dipping sauce you like.

Restaurant-style Roasted Vegetables

Servings: 4

Cooking: 25 Minutes

Ingredients:

- 1/2 teaspoon dried oregano
- 1/4 cup dry white wine
- 1/4 cup vegetable broth
- 1 red bell pepper, seeded and cut into 1/2-inch chunks
- 1 yellow bell pepper, seeded and cut into 1/2-inch chunks
- 1 yellow onion, quartered
- 1 green bell pepper, seeded and cut into 1/2-inch chunks
- 1 cup broccoli, broken into 1/2-inch florets
- 1/2 cup parsnip, trimmed and cut into 1/2-inch chunks
- 2 garlic cloves, minced
- Pink Himalayan salt and ground black pepper, to taste
- 1/2 teaspoon marjoram
- 1/2 cup Kalamata olives, pitted and sliced

Instructions

1. Place a single layer of your vegetables in the baking dish in the order that the colors of the rainbow appear. Garnish the vegetables with the minced garlic all around them.
2. Salt, black pepper, marjoram, and oregano should be used as seasonings. White wine and vegetable broth should be drizzled over the vegetables before serving.

3. Cook at a temperature of 0 degrees Fahrenheit for fifteen minutes in an Air Fryer that has been preheated, turning the pan once or twice.
4. Place the Kalamata olives in a sprinkling pattern over the vegetables, and serve warm. Bon appétit!

Almond Flour Battered 'n Crisped Onion Rings

Servings: 3
Cooking: 15 Minutes
Ingredients:

- 1 tablespoon baking powder
- 1 tablespoon smoked paprika
- ½ cup almond flour
- ¾ cup coconut milk
- 1 big white onion, sliced into rings
- 1 egg, beaten
- Salt and pepper to taste

Instructions

1. Turn on the air fryer and let it heat up for 5 minutes.
2. Almond flour, baking powder, smoked paprika, salt, and pepper should be mixed together in a bowl before using.
3. Eggs and coconut milk should be mixed together in a separate basin.
4. Coat the sliced onion in the egg mixture and set aside.
5. To prevent the onion slices from sticking, dredge them in the almond flour mixture.
6. Put the ingredients into the basket of the air fryer.
7. Cook for 15 minutes at 3250 degrees Fahrenheit with the lid closed.
8. Shake the frying basket halfway during the cooking period to ensure a consistent temperature throughout.

Crunchy Eggplant Rounds

Servings: 4

Cooking: 45 Minutes

Ingredients:

- 1/2 cup rice flour
- Coarse sea salt and ground black pepper, to taste
- 1 teaspoon paprika
- 1 cup water
- 1 cup cornbread crumbs, crushed
- 1 (1-pound) eggplant, sliced
- 1/2 cup flax meal
- 1/2 cup vegan parmesan

Instructions

1. Toss the eggplant with tablespoon of salt and let it stand for 30 minutes. Drain and rinse well.
2. Mix the flax meal, rice flour, salt, black pepper, and paprika in a bowl. Then, pour in the water and whisk to combine well.
3. In another shallow bowl, mix the cornbread crumbs and vegan parmesan.
4. Dip the eggplant slices in the flour mixture, then in the crumb mixture; press to coat on all sides. Transfer to the lightly greased Air Fryer basket.
5. Cook at 370 degrees F for 6 minutes. Turn each slice over and cook an additional minutes.
6. Serve garnished with spicy ketchup if desired. Bon appétit!

Crispy Ham Rolls

Servings: 3
Cooking: 17 Minutes
Ingredients:

- 3 packages Pepperidge farm rolls
- 1 tbsp softened butter
- 1 tsp mustard seeds
- 1 tsp poppy seeds
- 1 small chopped onion

Instructions

1. Mix butter, mustard, onion and poppy seeds. Spread the mixture on top of the rolls. Cover with the chopped ham. Roll up and arrange them on the basket of the air fryer; cook at 350 F for minutes.

Rice Flour Crusted Tofu

Servings: 3
Cooking: 28 Minutes
Ingredients:

- 1 (14-ounces) block firm tofu, pressed and cubed into ½-inch size
- 2 tablespoons cornstarch
- ¼ cup rice flour
- Salt and ground black pepper, as required
- 2 tablespoons olive oil

Instructions

1. In a bowl, mix together cornstarch, rice flour, salt, and black pepper.

2. Coat the tofu evenly with flour mixture.
3. Drizzle the tofu with oil.
4. Set the temperature of air fryer to 360 degrees F. Grease an air fryer basket.
5. Arrange tofu cubes into the prepared air fryer basket in a single layer.
6. Air fry for about 14 minutes per side.
7. Remove from air fryer and transfer the tofu onto serving plates.
8. Serve warm.

Swiss Cheese And Eggplant Crisps

Servings: 4

Cooking: 45 Minutes

Ingredients:

- 1/2 pound eggplant, sliced
- 1/4 cup almond meal
- 2 tablespoons flaxseed meal
- Coarse sea salt and ground black pepper, to taste
- 1 teaspoon paprika
- 1 cup parmesan, freshly grated

Instructions

1. Toss the eggplant with tablespoon of salt and let it stand for 30 minutes. Drain and rinse well.
2. Mix the almond meal, flaxseed meal, salt, black pepper, and paprika in a bowl. Then, pour in the water and whisk to combine well.
3. Then, place parmesan in another shallow bowl.
4. Dip the eggplant slices in the almond meal mixture, then in parmesan; press to coat on all sides. Transfer to the lightly greased Air Fryer basket.
5. Cook at 370 degrees F for 6 minutes. Turn each slice over and cook an additional minutes.

6. Serve garnished with spicy ketchup if desired. Bon appétit!

Open-faced Vegan Flatbread-wich

Servings: 4

Cooking: 25 Minutes

Ingredients:

- 1 can chickpeas, drained and rinsed
- 1 medium-sized head of cauliflower, cut into florets
- 1 tablespoon extra-virgin olive oil
- 2 ripe avocados, mashed
- 2 tablespoons lemon juice
- 4 flatbreads, toasted
- salt and pepper to taste

Instructions

1. Preheat the air fryer to 4250F.
2. In a mixing bowl, combine the cauliflower, chickpeas, olive oil, and lemon juice. Season with salt and pepper to taste.
3. Place inside the air fryer basket and cook for 25 minutes.
4. Once cooked, place on half of the flatbread and add avocado mash.
5. Season with more salt and pepper to taste.
6. Serve with hot sauce.

Cheese Pizza With Broccoli Crust

Servings: 1

Cooking: 30 Minutes

Ingredients:

- 3 cups broccoli rice, steamed

- ½ cup parmesan cheese, grated
- 1 egg
- 3 tbsp. low-carb Alfredo sauce
- ½ cup parmesan cheese, grated

Instructions

1. Drain the broccoli rice and combine with the parmesan cheese and egg in a bowl, mixing well.
2. Cut a piece of parchment paper roughly the size of the base of the fryer's basket. Spoon four equal-sized amounts of the broccoli mixture onto the paper and press each portion into the shape of a pizza crust. You may have to complete this part in two batches. Transfer the parchment to the fryer.
3. Cook at 0°F for five minutes. When the crust is firm, flip it over and cook for an additional two minutes.
4. Add the Alfredo sauce and mozzarella cheese on top of the crusts and cook for an additional seven minutes. The crusts are ready when the sauce and cheese have melted. Serve hot.

Chewy Glazed Parsnips

Servings: 6

Cooking: 44 Minutes

Ingredients:

- 2 pounds parsnips, peeled and cut into 1-inch chunks
- 1 tablespoon butter, melted
- 2 tablespoons maple syrup
- 1 tablespoon dried parsley flakes, crushed
- ¼ teaspoon red pepper flakes, crushed

Instructions

1. Preheat the Air fryer to 355 o F and grease an Air fryer basket.
2. Mix parsnips and butter in a bowl and toss to coat well.
3. Arrange the parsnips in the Air fryer basket and cook for about 40 minutes.
4. Meanwhile, mix remaining ingredients in a large bowl.
5. Transfer this mixture into the Air fryer basket and cook for about 4 more minutes.
6. Dish out and serve warm.

Herb Roasted Potatoes And Peppers

Servings: 4

Cooking: 30 Minutes

Ingredients:

1 pound russet potatoes, cut into 1-inch chunks

2 bell peppers, seeded and cut into 1-inch chunks

2 tablespoons olive oil

1 teaspoon dried rosemary

1 teaspoon dried basil

1 teaspoon dried oregano

1 teaspoon dried parsley flakes

Sea salt and ground black pepper, to taste

1/2 teaspoon smoked paprika

Instructions

Toss all ingredients in the Air Fryer basket.

Roast at 400 degrees F for 15 minutes, tossing the basket occasionally. Work in batches.

Serve warm and enjoy!

Hasselback Potatoes

Servings: 4

Cooking: 30 Minutes

Ingredients:

4 potatoes

2 tablespoons Parmesan cheese, shredded

1 tablespoon fresh chives, chopped

2 tablespoons olive oil

Instructions

Preheat the Air fryer to 355 o F and grease an Air fryer basket.

Cut slits along each potato about ¼-inch apart with a sharp knife, making sure slices should stay connected at the bottom.

Coat the potatoes with olive oil and arrange into the Air fryer basket.

Cook for about 30 minutes and dish out in a platter.

Top with chives and Parmesan cheese to serve.

Roasted Rosemary Squash

Servings: 2

Cooking: 30 Minutes

Ingredients:

1 tbsp dried rosemary

Cooking spray

Salt to season

Instructions

Place the butternut squash on a cutting board and peel it; cut it in half and remove the seeds. Cut the pulp into wedges and season with salt.

Preheat air fryer to 350 F, spray the squash with cooking spray and sprinkle with rosemary. Grease the fryer's basket with cooking spray and place the wedges inside. Slide the fryer basket back in and cook for minutes, flipping once halfway through. Serve with maple syrup and goat cheese.

Easy Granola With Raisins And Nuts

Servings: 8

Cooking: 40 Minutes

Ingredients:

2 cups rolled oats

1/2 cup walnuts, chopped

1/3 cup almonds chopped

1/4 cup raisins

1/4 cup whole wheat pastry flour

1/2 teaspoon cinnamon

1/4 teaspoon nutmeg, preferably freshly grated

1/2 teaspoon salt

1/3 cup coconut oil, melted

1/3 cup agave nectar

1/2 teaspoon coconut extract

1/2 teaspoon vanilla extract

Instructions

Thoroughly combine all ingredients. Then, spread the mixture onto the Air Fryer trays. Spritz with cooking spray.

Bake at 0 degrees F for 25 minutes; rotate the trays and bake 10 to 15 minutes more.

This granola can be stored in an airtight container for up to 2 weeks. Enjoy!

6

SNACKS & APPETIZERS RECIPES

Bacon-wrapped Cheese Croquettes

Servings: 6

Cooking: 8 Minutes

Ingredients:

- 3 eggs
- Salt, to taste
- 1cup all-purpose flour
- 1 cup breadcrumbs
- 1 tablespoon olive oil
- 1 pound thin bacon slices
- 1 pound sharp cheddar cheese block, cut into 1-inch rectangular pieces

Instructions

1. The air fryer should be preheated to 390 degrees Fahrenheit, and the basket should be greased.
2. Wrap one piece of cheddar cheese with bacon strips so that it is completely encased.
3. Repeat the previous step with the remaining cheese and bacon slices.

4. After arranging the croquettes in a baking tray, you will need to place them in the freezer for around ten minutes.
5. A shallow bowl is utilized to hold the flour.
6. Prepare the eggs in a separate bowl by whisking them.
7. In a third, more shallow dish, olive oil, breadcrumbs, and salt are mixed together.
8. First, the croquettes should be coated evenly in flour, and then they should be dipped in eggs.
9. After the croquettes have been coated in the breadcrumb mixture, place them in the basket of an air fryer.
10. Cook for about eight minutes, then serve the food while it is still warm.

Mexican Zucchini And Bacon Cakes Ole

Servings: 4

Cooking: 22 Minutes

Ingredients:

- 1/3 teaspoon fine sea salt
- 1/3 teaspoon baking powder
- 1/3 cup scallions, finely chopped
- 1/2 tablespoon fresh basil, finely chopped
- 1 zucchini, trimmed and grated
- 1/2 teaspoon freshly cracked black pepper
- 1 cup Cotija cheese, grated
- 1 teaspoon Mexican oregano
- 1 cup bacon, chopped
- 1/4 cup almond meal
- 1/4 cup coconut flour
- 2 small eggs, lightly beaten
- 1/3 cup Swiss cheese, grated

Instructions

1. Combine all of the ingredients, excluding the Cotija cheese, and stir until completely combined.
2. Then, gently press down on each ball to flatten it. The cakes should be sprayed with a cooking oil that is nonstick before baking.
3. Your cakes should be baked for one minute at 305 degrees Fahrenheit, and each batch should be done separately. Warm up this dish and serve it with some tomato ketchup and mayonnaise on the side.

Mozzarella Sticks

Servings: 4

Cooking: 60 Minutes

Ingredients:

- 1 tsp. dried parsley
- 2 eggs
- ½ oz. pork rinds, finely ground
- ½ cup parmesan cheese, grated
- 6 x 1-oz. mozzarella string cheese sticks

Instructions

1. After cutting the mozzarella sticks in half lengthwise, place them in the freezer for about half an hour. You have the option of leaving them in the freezer for a longer period of time and protecting them from freezer burn by placing them in a Ziploc bag.
2. Put the pork rinds, dried parsley, and parmesan in a small bowl and mix them together.
3. To beat the eggs, place them in a separate basin and use a fork.
4. Take a frozen mozzarella stick and coat it in eggs, then dip it in the pork rind mixture, being sure to cover it completely with the mixture. Continue rolling the remaining cheese sticks in the coating and placing them in the basket of the air fryer.

5. Cook for ten minutes at 400 degrees Fahrenheit, or until it reaches a golden brown color.
6. Serve with your own homemade marinara sauce on the side, if desired.

Simple Banana Chips

Servings: 8

Cooking: 10 Minutes

Ingredients:

- 2 tablespoons olive oil
- Salt and black pepper, to taste
- 2 raw bananas, peeled and sliced

Instructions

1. In order to be ready for using an air fryer, first grease the basket and then preheat the air fryer to 355 degrees Fahrenheit.
2. After coating them uniformly with oil, set the banana slices down in the basket of the air fryer.
3. After cooking for roughly ten minutes, season with salt and pepper before serving.
4. Dispense and serve hot.

Brussels Sprouts With Feta Cheese

Servings: 4

Cooking: 20 Minutes

Ingredients:

- 1 tablespoon lemon zest
- Non-stick cooking spray
- 1 cup feta cheese, cubed
- 3/4 pound Brussels sprouts, trimmed and cut off the ends
- 1 teaspoon kosher salt

Instructions

1. Peel the Brussels sprouts with a small paring knife at the beginning of the recipe. Salt and lemon zest are going to be sprinkled on the leaves before they are sprayed with cooking spray on all sides.
2. During the second half of the cooking time, give the cooking basket a shake, and continue baking at 380 degrees for another seven minutes.
3. Perform tasks in stages to guarantee that everything will be cooked properly. Make any necessary adjustments to the components. Alongside the salad, serve feta cheese. Bon appétit!

Cumin Pork Sticks

Servings: 4

Cooking: 12 Minutes

Ingredients:

- ½ teaspoon chili powder
- ¼ teaspoon ground cumin
- 1 teaspoon sunflower oil
- 8 oz pork loin
- 2 eggs, beaten
- 4 tablespoons flax meal

Instructions

1. Sticks of pork loin should be cut and seasoned with a combination of chili powder and cumin. Following this step, the skewers of pork are dipped in eggs and then coated in flax meal.
2. First, add some sunflower oil to the interior of the air fryer, and then add the meat.
3. Cook the snack for six minutes at a temperature of 400 degrees. After that, give the pork sticks another six minutes of cooking time after

turning them over.

Bell Pepper Chips

Servings: 4

Cooking: 20 Minutes

Ingredients:

- 1 egg, beaten
- 1/2 cup parmesan, grated
- 1 teaspoon sea salt
- 2 tablespoons grapeseed oil
- 1/2 teaspoon red pepper flakes, crushed
- 3/4 pound bell peppers, deveined and cut to 1/4-inch strips

Instructions

1. Combine the egg, the parmesan, the salt, and the crushed red pepper flakes in a mixing bowl until everything is well distributed.
2. Before putting the bell peppers in the cooking basket, coat them with batter and then do so. Apply a layer of grapeseed oil to the surface.
3. In an Air Fryer that has been preheated to temperature, the food is cooked for four minutes at 0 degrees Fahrenheit. Cooking will continue for another three minutes after the basket is shook. Collaborate with others.
4. Before serving, make sure to taste it and adjust the seasoning as necessary. Bon appétit!

Crunchy Bacon Bites

Servings: 4

Cooking: 10 Minutes

Ingredients:

- 1/4 cup hot sauce
- 4 bacon strips, cut into small pieces
- 1/2 cup pork rinds, crushed

Instructions

1. To a bowl, add bits of crumbled bacon.
2. The hot sauce should be added, and the ingredients should be completely combined.
3. Toss the crumbled pig rinds with the crumbled bacon until the bacon is equally coated with the pig rinds.
4. Cook the bacon in the air fryer for ten minutes at a temperature of 350 degrees Fahrenheit once you've transferred it to the basket.
5. Enjoy being of service to you customers.

Broccoli Fries With Spicy Dip

Servings: 4

Cooking: 15 Minutes

Ingredients:

Spicy Dip:

- 1 teaspoon granulated garlic
- 1/2 teaspoon cayenne pepper
- Sea salt and ground black pepper, to taste
- 2 tablespoons sesame oil
- 4 tablespoons parmesan cheese, preferably freshly grated
- 1 teaspoon hot sauce
- 1/4 cup mayonnaise
- 1/4 cup Greek yogurt
- 1/4 teaspoon Dijon mustard
- 3/4 pound broccoli florets
- 1/2 teaspoon onion powder

Instructions

1. To begin, preheat the Air Fryer to a temperature of 400 degrees Fahrenheit.
2. Broccoli should be cooked in salted water that is boiling for three to four minutes, or until it reaches the "al dente" stage. After thoroughly draining the food, transfer it to the basket of an Air Fryer that has been brushed with oil.
3. To the dish, incorporate the following ingredients: onion powder, garlic, cayenne pepper, salt, black pepper, sesame oil, and parmesan cheese.
4. Cook for six minutes, turning the food over after three minutes of cooking.
5. While that is going on, mix together all of the components of the spicy dip. A dipping sauce that has been chilled should be served with the broccoli fries. Bon appétit!

Spicy Dip

Servings: 6

Cooking: 5 Minutes

Ingredients:

- Pepper
- Salt
- 12 oz hot peppers, chopped
- 1 1/2 cups apple cider vinegar

Instructions

1. Combine all of the ingredients in the baking dish for the air fryer by stirring them.
2. Five minutes in the air fryer set to 380 degrees Fahrenheit for the cooking time.

3. Place the pepper combination in a blender and process until the mixture is perfectly smooth.
4. Feel free to serve with joy.

Crunchy Broccoli Fries

Servings: 4

Cooking: 15 Minutes

Ingredients:

- 1/2 teaspoon onion powder
- 1 teaspoon granulated garlic
- 1/2 teaspoon cayenne pepper
- 4 tablespoons parmesan cheese, preferably freshly grated
- Sea salt and ground black pepper, to taste
- 2 tablespoons sesame oil
- 1 pound broccoli florets

Instructions

1. To begin, preheat the Air Fryer to a temperature of 400 degrees Fahrenheit.
2. Broccoli should be cooked in salted water that is boiling for three to four minutes, or until it reaches the "al dente" stage. After thoroughly draining the food, transfer it to the basket of an Air Fryer that has been brushed with oil.
3. In a bowl, combine the onion powder, garlic, cayenne pepper, black pepper, and salt. Next, stir in the sesame oil.
4. Cook for six minutes, turning the food over after three minutes of cooking. Bon appétit!

Cheesy Zucchini Sticks

Servings: 2

Cooking: 20 Minutes

Ingredients:

- Sea salt and black pepper, to your liking
- 1 tablespoon garlic powder
- 1 zucchini, slice into strips
- 2 tablespoons mayonnaise
- 1/4 cup tortilla chips, crushed
- 1/4 cup Romano cheese, shredded
- 1/2 teaspoon red pepper flakes

Instructions

1. Cover zucchini in mayonnaise.
2. In a shallow dish, combine the crushed tortilla chips, cheese, and seasonings.
3. Then, coat the zucchini sticks with the cheese and potato chip mixture.
4. Cook at 0 degrees Fahrenheit for 12 minutes in an Air Fryer that has been warmed, shaking the basket halfway through the cooking time.
5. Work in batches until the sticks are golden brown and crisp. Bon appétit!

Bbq Lil Smokies

Servings: 6

Cooking: 20 Minutes

Ingredients:

- 1 pound beef cocktail wieners
- 10 ounces barbecue sauce, no sugar added

Instructions

1. Begin by heating the Air Fryer to 380 degrees Fahrenheit.

2. Using a fork, puncture your sausages and place them in the baking dish.
3. Cook for one minute Add the barbecue sauce to the pan and heat for two minutes more.
4. Serve food on toothpicks. Bon appétit!

Baby Corn

Servings: 4

Cooking: 20 Minutes

Ingredients:

- ½ tsp. carom seeds
- ¼ tsp. chili powder
- Pinch of baking soda
- 8 oz. baby corns, boiled
- 1 cup flour
- 1 tsp. garlic powder
- Salt to taste

Instructions

1. Combine the flour, chili powder, garlic powder, baking soda, salt, and caraway seed in a bowl. Add a small amount of water to form a batter-like consistency.
2. Coat each kernel with the batter.
3. At 0°F, preheat the Air Fryer.
4. Before placing the coated baby corn in the Air Fryer basket, cover the basket with aluminum foil.
5. Prepare for ten minutes.

Summer Meatball Skewers

Servings: 6

Cooking: 20 Minutes

Ingredients:

- Salt and black pepper, to taste
- 1 red pepper, 1-inch pieces
- 1 cup pearl onions
- 1/2 pound ground pork
- 1/2 pound ground beef
- 1 teaspoon dried onion flakes
- 1 teaspoon fresh garlic, minced
- 1 teaspoon dried parsley flakes
- 1/2 cup barbecue sauce

Instructions

1. Mix the ground meat with the onion flakes, garlic, parsley flakes, black pepper, and salt. Form the mixture into one-inch spheres.
2. Alternately thread the meatballs, pearl onions, and peppers onto skewers.
3. The barbecue sauce should be microwaved for 10 seconds.
4. 5 minutes at 380 degrees Fahrenheit in a preheated Air Fryer. Flip the skewers halfway through the grilling process. Apply the sauce and cook for an additional 5 minutes. Work in groups.
5. Enjoy with the remaining barbecue sauce.

Cauliflower Bombs With Sweet & Sour Sauce

Servings: 4

Cooking: 25 Minutes

Ingredients:

- 1 clove garlic, minced
- 1 teaspoon sherry vinegar
- 1 tablespoon tomato puree
- 2 tablespoons olive oil
- Cauliflower Bombs:
- 1/2 pound cauliflower

- 2 ounces Ricotta cheese
- 1/3 cup Swiss cheese
- 1 egg
- 1 tablespoon Italian seasoning mix
- Sweet & Sour Sauce:
- 1 red bell pepper, jarred
- Salt and black pepper, to taste

Instructions

1. Blanch the cauliflower for 3 to 4 minutes in salted boiling water until al dente. Drain thoroughly, then pulse in a food processor.
2. Add the remaining cauliflower bomb ingredients and thoroughly combine.
3. 16 minutes at 5 degrees Fahrenheit in an Air Fryer that has been preheated and shaken midway during cooking.
4. In the interim, mix all of the ingredients for the sauce in a food processor. Season as desired. Serve the cauliflower bombs alongside the Sweet and Sour Sauce. Bon appétit!

Fried Pickle Chips With Greek Yogurt Dip

Servings: 5

Cooking: 20 Minutes

Ingredients:

- 2 cups pickle chips, pat dry with kitchen towels
- Greek Yogurt Dip:
- 1/2 cup Greek yogurt
- 1 clove garlic, minced
- 1/4 teaspoon ground black pepper
- 1/2 cup cornmeal
- 1/2 cup all-purpose flour
- 1 teaspoon cayenne pepper

- 1/2 teaspoon shallot powder
- 1 teaspoon garlic powder
- 1/2 teaspoon porcini powder
- Kosher salt and ground black pepper, to taste
- 2 eggs
- 1 tablespoon fresh chives, chopped

Instructions

1. In a shallow dish, thoroughly combine the cornmeal and flour with the seasonings. Separately, beat the eggs in a small basin.
2. The pickle chips are dredged in the flour mixture and then the egg mixture. Press the pickle chips evenly into the flour mixture again.
3. Cook in a preheated Air Fryer at 400 degrees Fahrenheit for five minutes, then shake the basket and cook for an additional five minutes. Work in groups.
4. Meanwhile, thoroughly combine all of the ingredients for the sauce. Enjoy the fried pickles with the yogurt dip.

Old-fashioned Onion Rings

Servings: 4

Cooking: 10 Minutes

Ingredients:

- ¾ cup dry bread crumbs
- 1 large onion, cut into rings
- 1¼ cups all-purpose flour
- 1 cup milk
- 1 egg
- Salt, to taste

Instructions

1. Prepare the Air fryer to 360 degrees Fahrenheit and grease the basket.
2. Combine flour and salt in a bowl.
3. In a second dish, whisk egg with milk until completely combined.
4. Put the breadcrumbs in the last dish.
5. Coat the onion rings in the flour mixture, then dip them in the egg mixture.
6. Finally, dredge the onion rings in the breadcrumbs and place them to the Air fryer basket.
7. Cook for approximately 10 minutes and serve warm.

Cashew Dip

Servings: 6

Cooking: 8 Minutes

Ingredients:

- A pinch of salt and black pepper
- ½ cup cashews, soaked in water for 4 hours and drained
- 3 tablespoons cilantro, chopped
- 2 garlic cloves, minced
- 1 teaspoon lime juice
- 2 tablespoons coconut milk

Instructions

1. Combine all the ingredients in a blender, then transfer to a ramekin. Place the ramekin in the basket of your air fryer and cook at 350 degrees Fahrenheit for 8 minutes. Serve as a dip during a gathering.

Sweet Potato Bites

Servings: 2

Cooking: 30 Minutes

Ingredients:

- 2 tbsp. olive oil
- 2 tbsp. honey
- 2 sweet potatoes, diced into 1-inch cubes
- 1 tsp. red chili flakes
- 2 tsp. cinnamon
- ½ cup fresh parsley, chopped

Instructions

1. Pre-heat the Air Fryer to 350 degrees Fahrenheit.
2. In a bowl, combine all of the ingredients and whisk vigorously to evenly coat the sweet potato cubes.
3. Cook the sweet potato combination for 15 minutes in the Air Fryer basket.

Roasted Peanuts

Servings: 10

Cooking: 14 Minutes

Ingredients:

- 1 tablespoon olive oil
- Salt, as required
- 2½ cups raw peanuts

Instructions

1. Adjust the Air Fryer's temperature to 320 degrees Fahrenheit.
2. Add the peanuts to the basket of an Air Fryer in a single layer.
3. Air-fry for approximately 9 minutes, flipping twice.
4. Transfer the peanuts from the Air Fryer basket to a bowl.
5. Add the oil and salt, then toss to evenly coat.
6. Return the nut mixture to the basket of the Air Fryer.
7. Air-fry for roughly five minutes.

8. Transfer the finished nuts to a glass or metal bowl and serve them hot.

7

DESSERTS RECIPES

Ninja Pop-tarts

Servings: 6
Cooking: 1 Hour
Ingredients:

- Lemon Glaze:
- 1¼ cups powdered swerve
- 2 tablespoons lemon juice
- zest of 1 lemon
- 1 teaspoon coconut oil, melted
- Pop-tarts:
- 1 cup coconut flour
- 1 cup almond flour
- ½ cup of ice-cold water
- Pop-tarts:
- ¼ teaspoon salt
- 2 tablespoons swerve
- 2/3 cup very cold coconut oil
- ½ teaspoon vanilla extract

- ¼ teaspoon vanilla extract

Instructions

1. Pop-Tarts: Preheat the Air fryer to 375 degrees Fahrenheit and lubricate its basket.
2. In a bowl, combine the flours, swerve, and salt, then whisk in the coconut oil.
3. With a fork, thoroughly combine the almond meal until a mixture is formed.
4. Mix in the vanilla extract and 1 tablespoon of cold water until a firm dough forms.
5. Divide the dough into two equal portions and roll out into a thin sheet.
6. Cut each sheet into twelve rectangles of equal size, and place four rectangles in the Air fryer basket.
7. Cook for approximately ten minutes, then repeat with the remaining squares.
8. Lemon Glaze: In the meantime, combine all of the ingredients for the lemon glaze and drizzle it over the baked tarts.
9. Serve with sprinkles on top.

Zucchini Brownies

Servings: 12
Cooking: 35 Minutes
Ingredients:

- 1 teaspoon vanilla extract
- 1/3 cup applesauce, unsweetened
- 1 teaspoon ground cinnamon
- 1 cup butter
- 1 cup dark chocolate chips
- 1½ cups zucchini, shredded

- ¼ teaspoon baking soda
- 1 egg
- ½ teaspoon ground nutmeg

Instructions

1. Preheat the Air fryer to 345 degrees Fahrenheit and grease three large ramekins.
2. All the ingredients should be thoroughly blended in a big bowl.
3. Pour evenly into the prepared ramekins, then use the back of a spatula to level the surface.
4. Transfer the ramekin to the basket of the Air fryer and cook for approximately 35 minutes.
5. To serve, dish up and cut into slices.

Avocado Cake

Servings: 4
Cooking: 30 Minutes
Ingredients:

- 1 cup swerve
- 4 tablespoons butter, melted
- 4 ounces raspberries
- 2 avocados, peeled, pitted and mashed
- 1 cup almonds flour
- 3 teaspoons baking powder
- 4 eggs, whisked

Instructions

1. In a bowl, combine all the ingredients, toss, and then pour the mixture into an air fryer-compatible cake pan coated with parchment paper.

Cook at 340 degrees Fahrenheit for 30 minutes. Allow the cake to cool before slicing and serving.

Vanilla Pound Cake

Servings: 12
Cooking: 30 Minutes
Ingredients:

- 1/3 cup water
- 2/3 cup butter, melted
- ¼ teaspoon salt
- ½ cup erythritol powder
- 1 vanilla bean, scraped
- 4 large eggs

Instructions

1. Warm the air fryer for five minutes.
2. Combine all of the ingredients in a bowl.
3. Pour into a dish that has been buttered.
4. Bake at 3750F for 30 minutes in an air fryer.

Choco-coconut Puddin

Servings: 1
Cooking: 65 Minutes
Ingredients:

- ½ tbsp quality gelatin
- 1 cup coconut milk
- 2 tbsp cacao powder or organic cocoa
- ½ tsp Sugar powder extract or 2 tbsp honey/maple syrup

- 1 tbsp water

Instructions

1. Combine the coconut milk, cocoa, and sweetener over medium heat.
2. In a separate bowl, combine water and gelatin.
3. Add to the pan and stir until dissolved completely.
4. Pour into tiny plates and chill for one hour.
5. Serve!

Chocolate Molten Lava Cake

Servings: 4
Cooking: 25 Minutes
Ingredients:

- 1 ½ tbsp. flour
- 3 ½ oz. butter, melted
- 3 ½ tbsp. sugar
- 3 ½ oz. chocolate, melted
- 2 eggs

Instructions

1. Preheat the Air Fryer to 375 degrees Fahrenheit.
2. Lightly grease four ramekins with butter.
3. Combine the eggs and butter thoroughly before adding in the melted chocolate.
4. Fold in the flour gradually.
5. Each ramekin should get the same amount of the mixture.
6. Cook them in the Air Fryer for ten minutes.
7. Place the ramekins on plates inverted and let the cakes to fall out. Serve warm.

Nuts Cookies

Servings: 6

Cooking: 10 Minutes

Ingredients:

- ½ teaspoon baking powder
- 3 tablespoons Erythritol
- ½ cup butter, softened
- 1 cup coconut flour
- 3 oz macadamia nuts, grinded
- Cooking spray

Instructions

1. In a mixing dish, combine butter, coconut flour, coconut nut powder, Erythritol, and ground coconut. Knead the sticky-free dough. The dough is divided into small pieces that are then rolled into balls. Each cookie ball must be gently pressed to form cookies. Preheat the air fryer to 365 degrees Fahrenheit. Spray the basket of the air fryer with cooking spray. Cook the uncooked cookies in an air fryer for eight minutes. Then, heat for an additional two minutes at 390 degrees Fahrenheit to achieve a light brown crust.

Crème Brulee

Servings: 3

Cooking: 60 Minutes

Ingredients:

- 10 egg yolks
- 1 cup milk
- 2 vanilla pods

- 4 tbsp sugar + extra for topping

Instructions

1. Add the milk and cream to a pan. Cut open the vanilla pods and scrape the seeds into the pan along with the pods. Place the pan on the burner over medium heat and stir often until the liquid is nearly boiling. Turn the heat off. Add egg yolks to a bowl and whisk them. Add the sugar and blend thoroughly, but do not overmix.
2. Remove the vanilla pods from the milk mixture, then slowly pour the milk liquid into the egg mixture while still stirring. Let it settle for minutes. Fill between two and three ramekins with the ingredients. Place the ramekins in the fryer basket and cook them for 50 minutes at 190 degrees Fahrenheit. Once the ramekins are done, remove them and allow them to cool. Use a torch to melt the remaining sugar so that it caramelizes and browns on top.

Strawberry Pop Tarts

Servings: 6
Cooking: 25 Minutes
Ingredients:

- 1/3 cup low-sugar strawberry preserves
- 2 refrigerated pie crusts
- 1 oz reduced-fat Philadelphia cream cheese
- 1 tsp cornstarch
- 1 tsp stevia
- 1 tsp sugar sprinkles
- 1/2 cup plain, non-fat vanilla Greek yogurt
- olive oil or coconut oil spray

Instructions

1. Cut pie crusts into 6 equal rectangles.
2. Combine cornstarch and preserves in a bowl. Add preserves to the center of the crust. Fold the crust over. Fork-crimp edges to seal them. Continue with remaining crusts.
3. Spray the air fryer's baking pan lightly with cooking spray. Layer the pop tarts in a single layer. At 0°F, cook in batches for 8 minutes.
4. In the meantime, prepare the icing by combining stevia, cream cheese, and yogurt in a bowl. Spread on top of a baked pop tart and sprinkle with sugar.
5. Serve with pleasure.

Dark Chocolate Brownies

Servings: 10

Cooking: 35 Minutes

Ingredients:

- ¼ cup cocoa powder
- 1 cup chopped walnuts
- 6 oz butter
- ¾ cup white sugar
- 3 eggs
- 2 tsp vanilla extract
- ¾ cup flour
- 1 cup white chocolate chips

Instructions

1. In your air fryer, line a pan with baking paper. Melt chocolate and butter in a saucepan over low heat. Do not stop stirring until the mixture is smooth. Allow to slightly cool, then whisk in eggs and vanilla. Sift flour and cocoa, then stir to thoroughly combine. Incorporate the white chocolate and walnuts into the batter. Pour the batter into the pan and

bake at 340 degrees for 20 minutes. Serve accompanied by raspberry syrup and ice cream.

Nutella And Banana Pastries

Servings: 4

Cooking: 12 Minutes

Ingredients:

- 2 bananas, sliced
- 1 puff pastry sheet, cut into 4 equal squares
- ½ cup Nutella
- 2 tablespoons icing sugar

Instructions

1. Preheat the Air fryer to 375 degrees Fahrenheit and oil the basket.
2. Each pastry square is topped with Nutella, banana slices, and icing sugar.
3. Each square is folded into a triangle and the edges are delicately pressed with a fork.
4. Cook the pastries in the Air fryer basket for approximately 12 minutes.
5. Dispense and serve without delay.

Orange Swiss Roll

Servings: 6

Cooking: 1 Hour 20 Minutes

Ingredients:

- Filling:
- 2 tablespoons butter
- 4 tablespoons swerve

- 1 teaspoon ground star anise
- 1/4 teaspoon ground cinnamon
- 1 teaspoon vanilla paste
- 1/2 cup milk
- 1/4 cup swerve
- 1 tablespoon yeast
- 1/2 stick butter, at room temperature
- 1 egg, at room temperature
- 1/4 teaspoon salt
- 1 cup almond flour
- 1 cup coconut flour
- 2 tablespoons fresh orange juice
- 1/2 cup confectioners' swerve

Instructions

1. Warm the milk in a microwave-safe bowl before transferring it to the bowl of an electric stand mixer. Combine the four cups of swerve and yeast well. Cover and allow to ferment until the yeast is frothy.
2. Next, whip the butter slowly. Add the egg, then mix again. Add salt and flour. Mix the orange juice with the flour until a soft dough forms.
3. Knead the dough on a surface dusted with flour. Allow it to rest in a warm area for one hour, or until it has doubled in size. Then, spray cooking oil on the bottom and sides of a baking pan (butter flavored).
4. Roll out your dough into a rectangle shape.
5. Butter the dough with 2 tbsp. Combine 4 tablespoons of swerve, ground star anise, cinnamon, and vanilla in a mixing bowl; sprinkle equally over the dough.
6. Then, roll your dough into a log shape. Cut into equal rolls and set in the Air Fryer basket coated with parchment paper.
7. Bake at 350 degrees for 12 minutes, flipping halfway through. Sprinkle confectioners' sift and enjoy!

Egg Custard

Servings: 6

Cooking: 32 Minutes

Ingredients:

- 2 cups heavy whipping cream
- 1/2 tsp vanilla
- 2 egg yolks
- 3 eggs
- 1/2 cup erythritol
- 1 tsp nutmeg

Instructions

1. Preheat the air fryer to 325 degrees Fahrenheit.
2. Add all ingredients to a large mixing bowl and whisk until thoroughly blended.
3. Pour the custard mixture into the oiled baking dish, and then place it in the air fryer.
4. Prepare for 32 minutes.
5. Allow it to cool completely before refrigerating for 1-2 hours.
6. Serve with pleasure.

Creamy Rice Pudding

Servings: 6

Cooking: 20 Minutes

Ingredients:

- 1/3 cup sugar
- 1 tablespoon heavy cream
- 1 tablespoon butter, melted

- 7 ounces white rice
- 16 ounces milk
- 1 teaspoon vanilla extract

Instructions

1. Mix all ingredients thoroughly in an air fryer-compatible pan.
2. Put the pan in the fryer and cook for minutes at 360 degrees Fahrenheit.
3. Refrigerate the pudding, divide it into bowls, and serve it cool.

Peach Parcel

Servings: 2
Cooking: 15 Minutes
Ingredients:

- 1 tablespoon sugar
- Pinch of ground cinnamon
- 1 peach, peeled, cored and halved
- 1 cup prepared vanilla custard
- 2 puff pastry sheets
- 1 egg, beaten lightly
- 1 tablespoon whipped cream

Instructions

1. Preheat the Air fryer to 340 degrees Fahrenheit and grease the basket.
2. In the middle of each pastry sheet, place a tablespoon of vanilla custard and a peach half.
3. In a bowl, combine sugar and cinnamon, then sprinkle on the peach halves.
4. Form a package from the sheets by pinching the corners together, then put to the Air fryer basket.

5. Cook for approximately one minute, then top with whipped cream.
6. Serve alongside the remaining custard.

Vanilla Coconut Cheese Cookies

Servings: 15

Cooking: 12 Minutes

Ingredients:

- 3 tbsp cream cheese, softened
- 1/2 cup coconut flour
- 1 egg
- 1/2 tsp baking powder
- 1 tsp vanilla
- 1/2 cup swerve
- 1/2 cup butter, softened
- Pinch of salt

Instructions

1. Cream together butter, sweetener, and cream cheese in a bowl.
2. Add egg and vanilla, then beat until creamy and smooth.
3. Beat together coconut flour, salt, and baking powder until mixed. Cover and refrigerate for one hour.
4. Preheat the air fryer to 325 degrees Fahrenheit.
5. Create cookies from dough and cook them in an air fryer for 12 minutes.
6. Serve with pleasure.

Mom's Orange Rolls

Servings: 6

Cooking: 1 Hour 20 Minutes

Ingredients:

- Filling:
- 2 tablespoons butter
- 4 tablespoons white sugar
- 1 teaspoon ground star anise
- 1/4 teaspoon ground cinnamon
- 1 teaspoon vanilla paste
- 1/2 cup milk
- 1/4 cup granulated sugar
- 1 tablespoon yeast
- 1/2 stick butter, at room temperature
- 1 egg, at room temperature
- 1/4 teaspoon salt
- 2 cups all-purpose flour
- 2 tablespoons fresh orange juice
- 1/2 cup confectioners' sugar

Instructions

1. Warm the milk in a microwave-safe bowl before transferring it to the bowl of an electric stand mixer. Add sugar granules and yeast and thoroughly blend them. Cover and allow to ferment until the yeast is frothy.
2. Next, whip the butter slowly. Add the egg, then mix again. Add salt and flour. Mix the orange juice with the flour until a soft dough forms.
3. Knead the dough on a surface dusted with flour. Allow it to rest in a warm area for one hour, or until it has doubled in size. Then, spray the bottom and sides of a baking dish with butter-flavored cooking oil.
4. Roll out your dough into a rectangle shape.
5. Butter the dough with 2 tbsp. Combine the white sugar, ground star anise, cinnamon, and vanilla in a mixing bowl; sprinkle equally over the dough.
6. Then, roll your dough into a log shape. Cut into equal rolls and set in the Air Fryer basket coated with parchment paper.

7. Bake at 350 degrees for 12 minutes, flipping halfway through. Enjoy dusted with confectioners' sugar!

Vanilla Mozzarella Balls

Servings: 8

Cooking: 4 Minutes

Ingredients:

- 1 tablespoon butter
- 2 tablespoons swerve
- 1 teaspoon baking powder
- ½ teaspoon vanilla extract
- 2 eggs, beaten
- 1 teaspoon almond butter, melted
- 7 oz coconut flour
- 2 oz almond flour
- 5 oz Mozzarella, shredded
- Cooking spray

Instructions

1. In a bowl, combine butter and mozzarella. Melt the mixture in the microwave for -15 minutes, or until it is liquid. Then, incorporate almond and coconut flours. Add sugar and baking soda. Add vanilla extract next, then whisk the mixture. Work the soft dough with your hands. If the mixture is not sufficiently melted, microwave it for an additional two to five seconds. Combining almond butter and eggs in a bowl. Form eight balls out of the almond flour mixture, then roll them in the egg mixture. Preheat the air fryer to 400 degrees Fahrenheit. Spray the interior of the air fryer basket with cooking spray and arrange the bread rolls in a single layer. Toast the bread roll for four minutes, or until golden brown. Cool the baked dessert to room temperature

and, if preferred, sprinkle with Splenda.

Peach Slices

Servings: 4
Cooking: 40 Minutes
Ingredients:

- 2 tbsp. unsalted butter
- ¼ tsp. vanilla extract
- 4 cups peaches, sliced
- 2 – 3 tbsp. sugar
- 2 tbsp. flour
- ⅓ cup oats
- 1 tsp. cinnamon

Instructions

1. Combine the peach pieces, sugar, vanilla extract, and cinnamon in a large bowl. Place the mixture in an Air Fryer-compatible baking dish.
2. Prepare for minutes at 290°F.
3. Separately, combine the oats, flour, and unsalted butter.
4. Once the peach slices have finished cooking, sprinkle the butter mixture over them.
5. Additional ten minutes of cooking at 300 - 310°F.
6. Remove from the frying and let crisp for 5 to 10 minutes. Served with ice cream upon request.

Butter Crumble

Servings: 4
Cooking: 25 Minutes
Ingredients:

- 1 tablespoon cream cheese
- 1 teaspoon baking powder
- ½ cup coconut flour
- 2 tablespoons butter, softened
- 2 tablespoon Erythritol
- 3 oz peanuts, crushed
- ½ teaspoon lemon juice

Instructions

1. Mix coconut flour, butter, Erythritol, baking powder, and lemon juice in a mixing bowl. Stir the mixture until it becomes uniform. Then freeze it for several minutes. In the interim, combine peanuts and cream cheese. The frozen dough is grated. Line the mold of the air fryer with baking paper. Then, place and flatten one-half of the grated dough in the mold. It has a cream cheese concoction on top. The leftover dough is then sprinkled over the cream cheese mixture. Place the crumble-filled mold in the air fryer and cook it for 25 minutes at 330 degrees Fahrenheit.

8

OTHER AIR FRYER RECIPES

Dijon And Curry Turkey Cutlets

Servings: 4

Cooking: 30 Minutes + Marinating Time

Ingredients:

1/2 tablespoon Dijon mustard

1/2 teaspoon curry powder

Sea salt flakes and freshly cracked black peppercorns, to savor

1/3pound turkey cutlets

1/2 cup fresh lemon juice

1/2 tablespoons tamari sauce

Instructions

Set the air fryer to cook at 375 degrees. Then, put the turkey cutlets into a mixing dish; add fresh lemon juice, tamari, and mustard; let it marinate at least 2 hours.

Coat each turkey cutlet with the curry powder, salt, and freshly cracked black peppercorns; roast for minutes; work in batches. Bon appétit!

Egg Salad With Asparagus And Spinach

Servings: 4

Cooking: 25 Minutes + Chilling Time

Ingredients:

4 eggs

1 pound asparagus, chopped

2 cup baby spinach

1/2 cup mayonnaise

1 teaspoon mustard

1 teaspoon fresh lemon juice

Sea salt and ground black pepper, to taste

Instructions

Place the wire rack in the Air Fryer basket; lower the eggs onto the wire rack.

Cook at 0 degrees F for 15 minutes.

Transfer them to an ice-cold water bath to stop the cooking. Peel the eggs under cold running water; coarsely chop the hard-boiled eggs and set aside.

Increase the temperature to 0 degrees F. Place your asparagus in the lightly greased Air Fryer basket.

Cook for minutes or until tender. Place in a nice salad bowl. Add the baby spinach.

In a mixing dish, thoroughly combine the remaining ingredients. Drizzle this dressing over the asparagus in the salad bowl and top with the chopped eggs. Bon appétit!

Spicy Peppery Egg Salad

Servings: 3

Cooking: 20 Minutes + Chilling Time

Ingredients:

6 eggs

1 teaspoon mustard

1/2 cup mayonnaise

1 tablespoon white vinegar

1 habanero pepper, minced

1 red bell pepper, seeded and sliced

1 green bell pepper, seeded and sliced

1 shallot, sliced

Sea salt and ground black pepper, to taste

Instructions

Place the wire rack in the Air Fryer basket; lower the eggs onto the wire rack.

Cook at 0 degrees F for 15 minutes.

Transfer them to an ice-cold water bath to stop the cooking. Peel the eggs under cold running water; coarsely chop the hard-boiled eggs and set aside.

Toss with the remaining ingredients and serve well chilled. Bon appétit!

Famous Western Eggs

Servings: 6

Cooking: 20 Minutes

Ingredients:

6 eggs

3/4 cup milk

1 ounce cream cheese, softened

Sea salt, to your liking

1/4 teaspoon ground black pepper

1/4 teaspoon paprika

6 ounces cooked ham, diced

1 onion, chopped

1/3 cup cheddar cheese, shredded

Instructions

Begin by preheating the Air Fryer to 360 degrees F. Spritz the sides and bottom of a baking pan with cooking oil.

In a mixing dish, whisk the eggs, milk, and cream cheese until pale. Add the spices, ham, and onion; stir until everything is well incorporated.

Pour the mixture into the baking pan; top with the cheddar cheese.

Bake in the preheated Air Fryer for 12 minutes. Serve warm and enjoy!

Potato And Kale Croquettes

Servings: 6

Cooking: 9 Minutes

Ingredients:

4 eggs, slightly beaten

1/3 cup flour

1/3 cup goat cheese, crumbled

1 ½ teaspoons fine sea salt

4 garlic cloves, minced

1 cup kale, steamed

1/3 cup breadcrumbs

1/3teaspoon red pepper flakes

3 potatoes, peeled and quartered

1/3 teaspoon dried dill weed

Instructions

Firstly, boil the potatoes in salted water. Once the potatoes are cooked, mash them; add the kale, goat cheese, minced garlic, sea salt, red pepper flakes, dill and one egg; stir to combine well.

Now, roll the mixture to form small croquettes.

Grab three shallow bowls. Place the flour in the first shallow bowl.

Beat the remaining 3 eggs in the second bowl. After that, throw the breadcrumbs into the third shallow bowl.

Dip each croquette in the flour; then, dip them in the eggs bowl; lastly, roll each croquette in the breadcrumbs.

Air fry at 335 degrees F for 7 minutes or until golden. Tate, adjust for seasonings and serve warm.

Fluffy Omelet With Leftover Beef

Servings: 4

Cooking: 20 Minutes

Ingredients:

Non-stick cooking spray

1/2 pound leftover beef, coarsely chopped

2 garlic cloves, pressed

1 cup kale, torn into pieces and wilted

1 bell pepper, chopped

6 eggs, beaten

6 tablespoons sour cream

1/2 teaspoon turmeric powder

1 teaspoon red pepper flakes

Salt and ground black pepper, to your liking

Instructions

Spritz the inside of four ramekins with a cooking spray.

Divide all of the above ingredients among the prepared ramekins. Stir until everything is well combined.

Air-fry at 0 degrees F for 16 minutes; check with a wooden stick and return the eggs to the Air Fryer for a few more minutes as needed. Serve immediately.

Fruit Skewers With A Greek Flair

Servings: 2

Cooking: 10 Minutes

Ingredients:

6 strawberries, halved

1 banana, peeled and sliced

1/4 pineapple, peeled and cubed

1 teaspoon fresh lemon juice

1/4 cup Greek-Style yoghurt, optional

2 tablespoons honey

1 teaspoon vanilla

Instructions

Toss the fruits with lemon juice in a mixing dish. Tread the fruit pieces on skewers.

Cook at 340 degrees F for 5 minutes.

Meanwhile, whisk the Greek yogurt with the honey and vanilla. Serve the fruit skewers with the Greek sauce on the side. Bon appétit!

Cajun Turkey Meatloaf

Servings: 6

Cooking: 45 Minutes

Ingredients:

1 1/3 pounds turkey breasts, ground

½ cup vegetable stock

2 eggs, lightly beaten

1/2 sprig thyme, chopped

1/2 teaspoon Cajun seasonings

1/2 sprig coriander, chopped

½ cup seasoned breadcrumbs

2 tablespoons butter, room temperature

1/2 cup scallions, chopped

1/3 teaspoon ground nutmeg

1/3 cup tomato ketchup

1/2 teaspoon table salt

2 teaspoons whole grain mustard

1/3 teaspoon mixed peppercorns, freshly cracked

Instructions

Firstly, warm the butter in a medium-sized saucepan that is placed over a moderate heat; sauté the scallions together with the chopped thyme and coriander leaves until just tender.

While the scallions are sautéing, set your air fryer to cook at 365 degrees

F.

Combine all the ingredients, minus the ketchup, in a mixing dish; fold in the sautéed mixture and mix again.

Shape into a meatloaf and top with the tomato ketchup. Air-fry for 50 minutes. Bon appétit!

Spring Chocolate Doughnuts

Servings: 6

Cooking: 20 Minutes

Ingredients:

1 can (16-ounce can buttermilk biscuits

Chocolate Glaze:

1 cup powdered sugar

4 tablespoons unsweetened baking cocoa

2 tablespoon butter, melted

2 tablespoons milk

Instructions

Bake your biscuits in the preheated Air Fryer at 350 degrees F for 8 minutes, flipping them halfway through the cooking time.

While the biscuits are baking, make the glaze.

Beat the ingredients with whisk until smooth, adding enough milk for the desired consistency; set aside.

Dip your doughnuts into the chocolate glaze and transfer to a cooling rack to set. Bon appétit!

Double Cheese Mushroom Balls

Servings: 4

Cooking: 30 Minutes

Ingredients:

1 ½ tablespoons olive oil

4 ounces cauliflower florets

3 garlic cloves, peeled and minced

1/2 yellow onion, finely chopped

1 small-sized red chili pepper, seeded and minced

1/2 cup roasted vegetable stock

2 cups white mushrooms, finely chopped

Sea salt and ground black pepper, or more to taste

1/2 cup Swiss cheese, grated

1/4 cup pork rinds

1 egg, beaten

1/4 cup Romano cheese, grated

Instructions

Blitz the cauliflower florets in your food processor until they're crumbled (it is the size of rice).

Heat a saucepan over a moderate heat; now, heat the oil and sweat the cauliflower. garlic, onions, and chili pepper until tender.

Throw in the mushrooms and fry until they are fragrant and the liquid has almost evaporated.

Add the vegetable stock and boil for 18 minutes. Now, add the salt, black pepper, Swiss cheese pork rinds, and beaten egg; mix to combine.

Allow the mixture to cool completely. Shape the mixture into balls. Dip the balls in the grated Romano cheese. Air-fry the balls for 7 minutes at 400 degrees F. Bon appétit!

Crispy Wontons With Asian Dipping Sauce

Servings: 4

Cooking: 20 Minutes

Ingredients:

1 teaspoon sesame oil

3/4 pound ground beef

Sea salt, to taste

1/4 teaspoon Sichuan pepper

20 wonton wrappers

Dipping Sauce:

2 tablespoons low-sodium soy sauce

1 tablespoon honey

1 teaspoon Gochujang

1 teaspoon rice wine vinegar

1/2 teaspoon sesame oil

Instructions

Heat teaspoon of sesame oil in a wok over medium-high heat. Cook the ground beef until no longer pink. Season with salt and Sichuan pepper.

Lay a piece of the wonton wrapper on your palm; add the beef mixture in the middle of the wrapper. Then, fold it up to form a triangle; pinch the edges to seal tightly.

Place your wontons in the lightly greased Air Fryer basket. Cook in the preheated Air Fryer at 0 degrees F for 10 minutes. Work in batches.

Meanwhile, mix all ingredients for the sauce. Serve warm.

Bagel 'n' Egg Melts

Servings: 3

Cooking: 25 Minutes

Ingredients:

3 eggs

3 slices smoked ham, chopped

1 teaspoon Dijon mustard

1/4 cup mayonnaise

Salt and white pepper, to taste

3 bagels

3 ounces Colby cheese, shredded

Instructions

Place the wire rack in the Air Fryer basket; lower the eggs onto the wire rack.

Cook at 0 degrees F for 15 minutes.

Transfer them to an ice-cold water bath to stop the cooking. Peel the eggs under cold running water; coarsely chop them and set aside.

Combine the chopped eggs, ham, mustard, mayonnaise, salt, and pepper in a mixing bowl.

Slice the bagels in half. Spread the egg mixture on top and sprinkle with the shredded cheese.

Grill in the preheated Air Fryer at 3 degrees F for 7 minutes or until cheese is melted. Bon appétit!

Homemade Pork Scratchings

Servings: 10

Cooking: 50 Minutes

Ingredients:

1 pound pork rind raw, scored by the butcher

1 tablespoon sea salt

2 tablespoon smoked paprika

Instructions

Sprinkle and rub salt on the skin side of the pork rind. Allow it to sit for 30 minutes.

Roast at 380 degrees F for 8 minutes; turn them over and cook for a further 8 minutes or until blistered.

Sprinkle the smoked paprika all over the pork scratchings and serve. Bon appétit!

Breakfast Eggs With Swiss Chard And Ham

Servings: 2

Cooking: 20 Minutes

Ingredients:

2 eggs

1/4 teaspoon dried or fresh marjoram

2 teaspoons chili powder

1/3 teaspoon kosher salt

1/2 cup steamed Swiss Chard

1/4 teaspoon dried or fresh rosemary

4 pork ham slices

1/3 teaspoon ground black pepper, or more to taste

Instructions

Divide the Swiss Chard and ham among 2 ramekins; crack an egg into each ramekin. Sprinkle with seasonings.

Cook for 15 minutes at 335 degrees F or until your eggs reach desired texture.

Serve warm with spicy tomato ketchup and pickles. Bon appétit!

Filipino Ground Meat Omelet (tortang Giniling)

Servings: 3

Cooking: 20 Minutes

Ingredients:

1 teaspoon lard

2/3 pound ground beef

1/4 teaspoon chili powder

1/2 teaspoon ground bay leaf

1/2 teaspoon ground pepper

Sea salt, to taste

1 green bell pepper, seeded and chopped

1 red bell pepper, seeded and chopped

6 eggs

1/3 cup double cream

1/2 cup Colby cheese, shredded

1 tomato, sliced

Instructions

Melt the lard in a cast-iron skillet over medium-high heat. Add the ground beef and cook for 4 minutes until no longer pink, crumbling with a spatula.

Add the ground beef mixture, along with the spices to the baking pan. Now, add the bell peppers.

In a mixing bowl, whisk the eggs with double cream. Spoon the mixture over the meat and peppers in the pan.

Cook in the preheated Air Fryer at 355 degrees F for 10 minutes.

Top with the cheese and tomato slices. Continue to cook for minutes more or until the eggs are golden and the cheese has melted.

Baked Denver Omelet With Sausage

Servings: 5

Cooking: 14 Minutes

Ingredients:

3 pork sausages, chopped

8 well-beaten eggs

1 ½ bell peppers, seeded and chopped

1 teaspoon smoked cayenne pepper

2 tablespoons Fontina cheese

1/2 teaspoon tarragon

1/2 teaspoon ground black pepper

1 teaspoon salt

Instructions

In a cast-iron skillet, sweat the bell peppers together with the chopped pork sausages until the peppers are fragrant and the sausage begins to release liquid.

Lightly grease the inside of a baking dish with pan spray.

Throw all of the above ingredients into the prepared baking dish, including the sautéed mixture; stir to combine.

Bake at 3 degrees F approximately 9 minutes. Serve right away with the salad of choice.

Cauliflower And Manchego Croquettes

Servings: 4

Cooking: 15 Minutes

Ingredients:

1 cup Manchego cheese, shredded

1 teaspoon paprika

1 teaspoon freshly ground black pepper

1/2 tablespoon fine sea salt

1/2 cup scallions, finely chopped

1 pound cauliflower florets

2 tablespoons canola oil

2 teaspoons dried basil

Instructions

1. Blitz the cauliflower florets in a food processor until finely crumbed. Then, combine the broccoli with the rest of the above ingredients.
2. Then, shape the balls using your hands. Now, flatten the balls to make the patties.
3. Next, cook your patties at 0 degrees F approximately 10 minutes. Bon appétit!

Keto Rolls With Halibut And Eggs

Servings: 4

Cooking: 25 Minutes

Ingredients:

4 keto rolls

1 pound smoked halibut, chopped

4 eggs

1 teaspoon dried thyme

1 teaspoon dried basil

Salt and black pepper, to taste

Instructions

1. Cut off the top of each keto roll; then, scoop out the insides to make the shells.
2. Lay the prepared keto roll shells in the lightly greased cooking basket.
3. Spritz with cooking oil; add the halibut. Crack an egg into each keto roll shell; sprinkle with thyme, basil, salt, and black pepper.
4. Bake in the preheated Air Fryer at 325 degrees F for 20 minutes. Bon appétit!

Country-style Apple Fries

Servings: 4

Cooking: 20 Minutes

Ingredients:

1/2 cup milk

1 egg

1/2 all-purpose flour

1 teaspoon baking powder

4 tablespoons brown sugar

1 teaspoon vanilla extract

1/2 teaspoon ground cloves

A pinch of kosher salt

A pinch of grated nutmeg

1 tablespoon coconut oil, melted

2 Pink Lady apples, cored, peeled, slice into pieces (shape and size of French fries

1/3 cup granulated sugar

1 teaspoon ground cinnamon

Instructions

1. In a mixing bowl, whisk the milk and eggs; gradually stir in the flour; add the baking powder, brown sugar, vanilla, cloves, salt, nutmeg, and

melted coconut oil. Mix to combine well.

2. Dip each apple slice into the batter, coating on all sides. Spritz the bottom of the cooking basket with cooking oil.
3. Cook the apple fries in the preheated Air Fryer at 5 degrees F approximately 8 minutes, turning them over halfway through the cooking time.
4. Cook in small batches to ensure even cooking.
5. In the meantime, mix the granulated sugar with the ground cinnamon; sprinkle the cinnamon sugar over the apple fries. Serve warm.

Italian Creamy Frittata With Kale

Servings: 3

Cooking: 20 Minutes

Ingredients:

1 yellow onion, finely chopped

6 ounces wild mushrooms, sliced

6 eggs

1/4 cup double cream

1/2 teaspoon cayenne pepper

Sea salt and ground black pepper, to taste

1 tablespoon butter, melted

2 tablespoons fresh Italian parsley, chopped

2 cups kale, chopped

1/2 cup mozzarella, shredded

Instructions

1. Begin by preheating the Air Fryer to 360 degrees F. Spritz the sides and bottom of a baking pan with cooking oil.
2. Add the onions and wild mushrooms, and cook in the preheated Air Fryer at 360 degrees F for 4 to 5 minutes.
3. In a mixing dish, whisk the eggs and double cream until pale. Add the spices, butter, parsley, and kale; stir until everything is well

incorporated.

4. Pour the mixture into the baking pan with the mushrooms.
5. Top with the cheese. Cook in the preheated Air Fryer for 10 minutes. Serve immediately and enjoy!

Sweet Mini Monkey Rolls

Servings: 6

Cooking: 25 Minutes

Ingredients:

3/4 cup brown sugar

1 stick butter, melted

1/4 cup granulated sugar

1 teaspoon ground cinnamon

1/4 teaspoon ground cardamom

1 (16-ounce) can refrigerated buttermilk biscuit dough

Instructions

1. Spritz 6 standard-size muffin cups with nonstick spray. Mix the brown sugar and butter; divide the mixture between muffin cups.
2. Mix the granulated sugar with cinnamon and cardamom. Separate the dough into 16 biscuits; cut each in 6 pieces. Roll the pieces over the cinnamon sugar mixture to coat. Divide between muffin cups.
3. Bake at 0 degrees F for about 20 minutes or until golden brown. Turn upside down and serve.

Dinner Avocado Chicken Sliders

Servings: 4

Cooking: 10 Minutes

Ingredients:

½ pounds ground chicken meat

4 burger buns

1/2 cup Romaine lettuce, loosely packed

½ teaspoon dried parsley flakes

1/3 teaspoon mustard seeds

1 teaspoon onion powder

1 ripe fresh avocado, mashed

1 teaspoon garlic powder

1 ½ tablespoon extra-virgin olive oil

1 cloves garlic, minced

Nonstick cooking spray

Salt and cracked black pepper (peppercorns, to taste

Instructions

Firstly, spritz an air fryer cooking basket with a nonstick cooking spray.

Mix ground chicken meat, mustard seeds, garlic powder, onion powder, parsley, salt, and black pepper until everything is thoroughly combined. Make sure not to overwork the meat to avoid tough chicken burgers.

Shape the meat mixture into patties and roll them in breadcrumbs; transfer your burgers to the prepared cooking basket. Brush the patties with the cooking spray.

Air-fry at 355 F for 9 minutes, working in batches. Slice burger buns into halves. In the meantime, combine olive oil with mashed avocado and pressed garlic.

To finish, lay Romaine lettuce and avocado spread on bun bottoms; now, add burgers and bun tops. Bon appétit!

9

CONCLUSION

The Gourmia air fryer is a very well-liked piece of cooking equipment now available on the market. It is the most effective way to cook scrumptious dishes that are also high in nutrients. When you want to make something tasty and savory for your loved ones, but you don't have the time, expertise, or stamina to spend hours in the kitchen, this is just what you need. Your cooking methods are about to be completely transformed, and the Gourmia air fryer will quickly become your new best buddy in the kitchen. If you already have such a practical piece of kitchen equipment, then the only thing missing from your life is this amazing collection of recipes. These fantastic journals are filled with mouthwatering recipes that are sure to blow your mind. They can all be made in a short amount of time and with minimal effort using the Gourmia air fryer, which calls for only basic, easily obtainable materials. That being said, get to work right away! For the convenience of cooking gourmet meals without having to leave the house, consider purchasing a Gourmia air fryer.

10

MEASUREMENT CONVERSION CHART

Gas Mark	° Celsius	° Celsius Fan	° Fahrenheit
¼	110°c	100°c	225°F
½	130°c	120°c	250°F
1	140°c	130°c	275°F
2	150°c	140°c	300°F
3	170°c	155°c	325°F
4	180°c	165°c	350°F
5	190°c	180°c	375°F
6	200°c	190°c	400°F
7	220°c	200°c	425°F
8	230°c	210°c	450°F
9	240°c	220°c	475°F

11

ABOUT THE AUTHOR

Michelle Turner is an expert in the fields of gastronomy, viniculture, and travel. She has worked in the field of food and wine for over a dozen years now and has a wealth of expertise. Recipes, ideas for food and wine pairings, and travel guides for food and wine are some of the things that she posts as a guest blogger on other people's blogs. She is a mother of three adolescents, and one of her goals is to create scrumptious, elevated, daily recipes and simple meal plans that any home cook can make in less time, with fewer ingredients, and a whole lot of love. She wants to share these with other home cooks so that they can pass them on to their own families.

Made in the USA
Monee, IL
24 May 2023

34445277R00116